JACOB

Levi Meier, Ph.D.

UNIVERSITY
PRESS OF
AMERICA

Lanham • New York • London

Copyright © 1994 by
University Press of America,® Inc.
4720 Boston Way
Lanham, Maryland 20706

3 Henrietta Street
London WC2E 8LU England

All rights reserved
Printed in the United States of America
British Cataloging in Publication Information Available

Library of Congress Cataloging-in-Publication Data
Meier, Levi.
Jacob / Levi Meier.
p.   cm.
Includes bibliographical references.
1. Jacob (Biblical patriarch)   2. Bible. O.T. Genesis—Biography.
I. Title.
BS580.J3M45   1994   222'.11'092—dc20   94–22335 CIP
[B]

ISBN 0–8191–9667–3 (cloth : alk. paper)
ISBN 0–8191–9668–1 (pbk. : alk. paper)

 The paper used in this publication meets the minimum requirements of American National Standard for Information Sciences—Permanence of Paper for Printed Library Materials, ANSI Z39.48–1984.

DEDICATION

with love
to my brother, my teacher,
Menahem

BS
580
.J3
M45
1994

PREFACE

I use my active imagination in suggesting what Jacob may have experienced in his soul throughout his lifetime. I also use my own voice to interpret some of Jacob's feelings, thoughts and actions. However, there are places where the reader may wonder where Jacob's monologue ends, and the voice of the author begins. I also wrestle with that same issue.

CONTENTS

Page

Preface

Contents

Introduction

Chapter I.	Jacob and his Four Wives	1
Chapter II.	God's Struggle with Man: Jacob and the Lonely Night Journey	33
Chapter III.	Jacob and "Hear, O Israel"	59
Chapter IV.	As Jacob is Touched by his Father	76
Chapter V.	Secrets of the Heart: Jacob's Blessings	91
Conclusion		108
References		112
About the Author		113

INTRODUCTION

My father died on Thursday, November 23, 1972 (corresponding to the Hebrew date of 17 Kislev, 5733) at the age of 58. He passed away in New York and was buried in Israel. It seems ironic that he died on Thanksgiving, a day that he enjoyed so much during his adult life. Together with my mother, he used to help prepare a delicious Thanksgiving dinner for our family and friends. Our family had grown that year. I had been married for one year, and my wife and I had just been blessed with our firstborn, our daughter Chana.

The Torah reading for the Sabbath following my father's passing dealt with Jacob's existential crisis, his lonely night journey of the soul prior to his meeting and reconciliation with his archenemy, his brother, Esau. Each year, I commemorate my father's Yahrzeit (anniversary of the day he died) when this same Torah portion is read in the synagogue. This reading causes me to focus intensely on Jacob's life, particularly the time when he was alone (Genesis 32:25). I continue to learn a great deal about Jacob and, in the process, about my father and myself.

My father's death was the first loss of a member of my immediate family. My grandfather had died fifteen years earlier, but with the loss of my father, my brother and I moved up one generation to a new position in the family, and I became more aware of my own mortality. For me, this loss precipitated my own lonely night journey of the soul, a period of trials and tribulations, which all human beings go through at one time or another. I was already a rabbi, married and a father. Despite my apparent security and sense of self, I suddenly experienced life with a sense of inner loneliness and existential insecurity, recognizing with greater clarity the finite nature of my existence.

As the years went by, I became more and more fascinated by Jacob's complex life. I felt that my father's death indirectly guided and gave birth to my passionate involvement in Jacob's life. It was as if our Patriarch Jacob became my spiritual father and guide. Through study,

INTRODUCTION

learning, meditation and active imagination, I began to explore many aspects of Jacob's life.

This passion entered into nearly all aspects of my life. I began to write and to explore art. My first painting, "Jacob's Ladder," now hangs over my bed, serving as a catalyst and guide for my rich dream life. My writing has allowed me to dialogue with Jacob, wrestle with him and adopt him as my soul mate. This process continues to be a deeply religious experience for me.

The Torah contains letters, words, sentences and paragraphs, all written down by a scribe. Yet, the *spaces* surrounding each letter and word afford the reader the opportunity to amplify and speculate on what surrounds the words of the text. I continue to explore those spaces through a process of meditation and active imagination.

Active imagination is a way of bringing something to life through dialogue and amplification. This process, similar to dreaming with open eyes, involves one's conscious participation in images, dreams and fantasies. The Bible is referred to as *Torat Hayim*, a living Torah. A living Torah demands that each individual, in every generation, capture, develop and ultimately bring to life the stories and personalities of the Bible. Every story must speak to each person and allow him or her to feel the living presence of all the Biblical characters.

Of all the Patriarchs and Matriarchs, Jacob seems to have led the most complex life. Indeed, his was one of the most complicated lives in Jewish history. Some of the difficulties that Jacob experienced relate to his *developmental process*. His problems seemingly began prior to his conception and continued throughout his life -- while he was *in utero*, during his childhood, young adulthood, married life and old age.

Even before Jacob was conceived, his parents faced enormously difficult events that were to have a later effect on him. His father, Isaac, was almost sacrificed to God by *his* father, Abraham. When Isaac eventually married, he and his wife, Rebekah, were childless for 20 years.

JACOB

When Rebekah finally conceived, her pregnancy was difficult, so that even Jacob's gestation period did not proceed smoothly. Jacob and his twin, Esau, were apparently incompatible even *in utero*. The incompatibility between these two very different sons, destined to become two different nations, seems to have begun during Rebekah's pregnancy. At the time of their birth, the twins began to "wrestle" with one another, as each struggled to come out of the womb first. Esau succeeded, but Jacob held on to his heel, showing his intense desire to be the firstborn.

During Jacob's childhood, he confronted the pain of sibling rivalry and parental favoritism. He received a special measure of love from his mother, while his father seemed particularly pleased with Esau, Jacob's polar opposite. Furthermore, although Jacob was "the whole man dwelling in tents" (Genesis 25:27), upholding high ethical standards, he found it necessary to take advantage of his brother's fatigue in order to purchase Esau's birthright.

In addition to the developmental issues that confronted Jacob, he contended with a number of *difficult relationships*. His interactions with his brother Esau were particularly problematic. He and Esau espoused different values and interests throughout their lives. Esau married two women, Judith and Basemath, who practiced idolatry, while Jacob remained faithful to the ways of his fathers.

Jacob resorted to deception, pretending that he was Esau, in order to receive Isaac's paternal blessing. Jacob's deception was carried out at the suggestion of his mother, who, prior to the twins' birth, received the Divine revelation that Esau, her firstborn, would be subordinate to Jacob, his younger brother. Esau's wrath was kindled after Jacob seemingly tricked him twice, first buying his birthright and then, receiving his blessing by deceptive means. Esau felt betrayed, and Jacob had to flee for his life.

Even when Jacob reached the safety of another land, Haran, his troubles continued. He himself became the victim of deception. Laban, Jacob's uncle and father-in-law, tricked him into marrying Leah instead of her twin sister, Rachel, whom Jacob loved. Jacob eventually married Rachel also, but she was infertile for a long time. His less loved wife,

INTRODUCTION

Leah, bore him many children while Rachel suffered the pain of childlessness. Meanwhile, Laban continued to deceive Jacob, cheating him out of wages and benefits that he had promised to bestow.

Jacob finally reconciled with his brother Esau, bringing an end to years of hatred and hiding. Before their reconciliation, Jacob endured an event that left him changed both physically and psychically. All alone, Jacob wrestled with an *Ish*, a Divine being, who blessed him and gave him the alternate name of Israel, but also dislocated his thigh. When Jacob finally found some peace in his relationship with his brother, he was confronted with a new family trauma. His only daughter, Dinah, was raped by Shechem, resulting in a bloody massacre of Shechem's town, led by Dinah's brothers, Simeon and Levi. Jacob still found no peace. When he was told that Joseph, his favorite son, had been killed by a wild beast, he mourned bitterly.

Jacob's life dealt primarily with his complex, and sometimes deceptive relationships with his father, mother, brother, wives, children and father-in-law. His soul also grappled with the many challenging experiences of his life, such as infertility, his work experience during the time that he lived with his father-in-law, Laban, and his illness at a late stage of his life.

This overview outlines the known facts about Jacob's external life. However, while he experienced each of these trials, Jacob struggled with his own inner life, his own psyche. He wrestled with tumultuous feelings about himself and his destiny, the nature of his own persona, and his relationships with his brother, parents, wives, children and grandchildren.

Undoubtedly, all of these experiences caused Jacob anguish, torment, fear and trepidation, as well as anxiety and depression. Any *one* of these many events would be capable of causing great emotional turmoil and difficulty; how much more so, the totality of these occurrences.

JACOB

Jacob's Psychic Reality

Jacob's psychic reality was very different from his physical reality. What perhaps gave Jacob the resilience and courage to confront all of these challenges was his perception of another reality, so different, promising, comforting and Divinely inspired, that it filled him with feelings of ecstasy. Jacob's inner strength flowed from his very personal relationship with the Image of God.

Jacob had three special, spiritual experiences, each of which took place at night. God chose to appear to Jacob and establish an intimate relationship with him, specifically during times of darkness, creating hopeful visions for his future. The psychic reality of these experiences sustained Jacob throughout his life.

The first event, Jacob's dream about the Ladder of Ascension, profoundly affected his inner life. This experience took place after Jacob's double "betrayal" of Esau -- his purchase of the birthright and receipt of the paternal blessing. Jacob feared that Esau would kill him out of hatred and jealousy. Jacob fled from Beersheba toward Haran, and on his way there, he encountered a new psychic reality that would forever change him.

At a resting-place on Jacob's journey to Haran, he dreamt of a Ladder of Ascension, extending from heaven to earth, with angels ascending and descending the rungs. During the course of this nighttime vision, God appeared to Jacob and proclaimed: "In you and in your seed, shall all the families of the earth be blessed," thus confirming His earlier promise to Abraham. He also added that "I am with you and will guard you wherever you go...I will not leave you" (Genesis 28:14-15). This supreme promise of God's constant Presence and blessing thereby became the central motif of Jacob's inner life, his psychic reality. His personal closeness to the Image of a comforting God sustained him during his journey, his years in Haran, and the ordeals that confronted him throughout his life.

Jacob's second, pivotal encounter with the Divine Presence, leading to an enhanced psychic reality, occurred prior to his reconciliation with

INTRODUCTION

Esau. Once again, this event took place at night, when Jacob remained completely alone (Genesis 32:25). Jacob encountered an *Ish*, an angel or Divine messenger, and wrestled with him until the break of day. During this struggle, the *Ish* gave Jacob a new name, Israel, indicating that Jacob would be able to deal with any adversary and *prevail*. This promise was both comforting and empowering, diminishing Jacob's fear of meeting Esau, as well as all other future confrontations. Jacob summarized this life-changing experience by commenting that "I have seen God face to face, and my life is preserved" (Genesis 32:31). Jacob knew that he had a unique, personal relationship with God, and that he would feel protected wherever he went. He would never *feel* completely alone.

Jacob's third major experience of the Divine took place before he went down to Egypt to be reunited with Joseph. God spoke to Jacob during another nighttime vision, saying: "Do not fear to go down to Egypt...I will go down with you, and I will surely bring you up again, and Joseph will put his hand upon your eyes" (Genesis 46:2-4). Once again, God promised His constant and continued Presence and protection. He comforted Jacob by stating that at Jacob's death, Joseph would be present to close his father's eyes, assuring Jacob of his son's continuing devotion and family continuity.

These three great life events gave Jacob the inner strength and stamina to face whatever befell him in life. He knew that he had a personal relationship with a loving, caring, comforting God who would never leave him and who would guide him all the days of his life. This psychic reality was as significant in Jacob's life as the physical realities that were summarized above in Jacob's "external" biography.

Jacob's inner and outer lives serve as instructive models for each of us, his descendants. Most people do not share their innermost secrets, the realities of their inner lives that constitute the major part of their existence. We are fortunate that the Torah presents us with a comprehensive picture of Jacob, his triumphs, his troubles and his secrets. By studying his life in depth, we can learn, as he did, that God's eternal Presence can give us the strength to proceed. Even one experience of the Divine may sustain us along our own journeys. When we truly incorporate the lessons of Jacob's life into our own experiences, we can say, along with the Psalmist (23:4): "...though I walk through the valley of the shadow of death, I will not fear evil, because You are with me..."

Jacob, our Father, Still Lives

I have attempted to integrate the two realities of Jacob's life, physical and psychic. I have utilized meditation, active imagination, dialogue and prayer to try to better understand the external and internal realities of Jacob's life. Each of us is capable of creating an ongoing dialogue between our inner and outer realities, and by so doing, we can produce life-sustaining energy. This ongoing dialogue thus enables us to undertake our individual life journeys.

In each of the chapters that follow, I examine major events in Jacob's life based on my understanding of his physical and psychic realities. Chapter I, "Jacob and His Four Wives," examines the complex relationships between Jacob and the four women in his life, Rachel, Leah, Bilhah and Zilpah, looking at issues of intimacy and family roles. What are the implications of a woman's role as concubine rather than wife? How does one deal with a beloved wife and one who is less loved, particularly when the less loved wife bears most of the children in the family?

In Chapter II, "God's Struggle with Man: Jacob and the Lonely Night Journey," I look at Jacob's encounter with an *Ish*, an angel or Divine messenger. That struggle is prototypical of all human struggles with different Images of God. Furthermore, I explore the nature of the "lonely night journey" that each of us undertakes at one time or another, as we strive to integrate the opposing qualities -- the Jacob and Esau elements -- that reside in each of us. We all struggle with our own Esau-like qualities, which we often project onto others. Only when we recognize these traits and confront the internal Esau can we deal with external manifestations of Esau.

Chapter III, "Jacob and 'Hear, O Israel'," analyzes Judaism's central declaration of faith. One interpretation of this sacred prayer regards it as a proclamation by Jacob's "children," i.e., all of us, to Jacob on his

INTRODUCTION

deathbed. By affirming this central Jewish belief on a daily basis, and acting upon it, we provide continuity from one generation to the next, fulfilling God's promise to Jacob. At many points during Jacob's lifetime, he wondered how he would achieve continuity of his family and his spiritual legacy. For him, as well as for each of us, continuity represents a form of immortality.

Chapter IV, "As Jacob Is Touched by His Father," examines the position and role of the firstborn. This status reflects each person's covenantal relationship with God and the inheritance of spirituality along with earthly possessions. Is being a firstborn merely a question of birth order? Or, is this status available to each child in every family? Despite the different characteristics that each of us possesses, can we all be firstborns? Can we all be special? Can we all be heirs to Jacob's spiritual legacy?

Chapter V, "Secrets of the Heart: Jacob's Blessings," is a meditation on the context and nature of Jacob's farewell blessings to his children. Jacob's blessing of Reuben is analyzed in detail, showing that it focuses on the pivotal role of sexuality in the lives of individuals and communities. Families' secret, sexual issues frequently involve aspects of incest. In all areas of sexual conflict, the individual struggles with his or her instinctual feelings and drives.

This book deals primarily with dialogue and struggle, i.e., the ongoing interaction between the physical and psychic realms. While these entities appear distinct, perhaps even dissonant, they are interdependent parts of a whole. The goal of lifetime dialogue and struggle is the refinement and purification of these two worlds so that they become one. We each weave a tapestry between these two spheres throughout our life journey. We try to achieve oneness through active imagination, meditation and prayer. However, the pursuit of oneness always allows for ambiguity, paradox and mystery.

The Talmud states (*Berakhot* 4a) that Jacob's fear prior to meeting Esau (Genesis 32:8) indicates his lack of trust in God's promise to constantly protect him. Jacob's emotions may also be understood by

JACOB

examining the very real, difficult circumstances of his life. Jacob's ongoing *struggle* allows us to examine the various issues in his life, dialogue with his psyche and apply what we learn to our own experience.

The boundaries of the psyche are permeable in both directions. The external experience and the inner experience have a mutual effect on one another. The physical and psychic worlds are equally real. To regard them as separate entities is ultimately an illusion. The concepts of visible and invisible worlds are artificial, created by our intellect to explain phenomena in terms that we can understand.

In reality, each of us exists in a unique world, and our goal is to find harmony as we discover the oneness of our existence. The last word of the *Shema* ("Hear, O Israel"), the Jewish declaration of faith, is *Ehad*, "one," indicating that the pursuit of oneness is the goal of our life journey.

The Talmud teaches us that Jacob, our father, has not died (*Taanit* 5b). Each of us continues Jacob's lifelong struggle for oneness and unity. On each anniversary of my own father's death, I am drawn to explore Jacob's inner and outer realities and his striving for oneness. Jacob thus serves as my spiritual father and mentor. Through this process of exploration and understanding, we can each come to regard Jacob as our father. Jacob, our father, still lives. By exploring Jacob's life, each of us can similarly gain insight into his conflicts, as well as our own.

Each of us can use Jacob's journey as a point of departure for exploring our lives and the lives of our parents, brothers, sisters, sons, daughters, other relatives and friends. Understanding the struggles of my father's life, his triumphs and disappointments, continues to give me insight into his life, and mine. Not only on the anniversary of my father's death, but also each day of my life, I am aware that, like Jacob, my father still lives.

CHAPTER I

JACOB AND HIS FOUR WIVES

I

INTRODUCTION

A striking omission in the traditional listing of our Matriarchs -- Sarah, Rebekah, Rachel and Leah -- is the absence of Bilhah and Zilpah from this list, despite the fact that they were the mothers of four of the twelve children (Dan, Naftali, Gad and Asher) who became the Twelve Tribes of Israel. This omission is strikingly noticeable in the blessing that parents give their daughters: "May God cause you to become like Sarah, Rebekah, Rachel and Leah;" Bilhah and Zilpah are excluded. We really know very little about Bilhah and Zilpah, though they were the mothers of a third of the Tribes of Israel.

Moreover, our knowledge of the lives of the four Matriarchs is limited. There is no mention of Rebekah's or Leah's death in the Biblical text. By contrast, Sarah's death and burial are recounted at length in Chapter 23 of Genesis. Rachel's death is also very poignantly presented. She died as she was giving birth to her youngest child, Benjamin. Indeed, the Hebrew name that Rachel proposes for the child, *Ben Oni*, "the son of my sorrow," reflects Rachel's suffering and subsequent death (Genesis 35:18-19). Yet, Jacob calls the boy Benjamin, "the son of my right hand," or "the son of my old age." Jacob seemingly ignores Rachel's deathbed request regarding their son's name. Years later, as Jacob is dying, he still vividly and poignantly recalls the death of his beloved Rachel (Genesis 48:7).

Although the deaths of Rebekah and Leah are not described, their burial sites are recorded as being in the Cave of Machpelah (Genesis 49:31), the same place that Sarah is buried. Rebekah's death is alluded to in the mention of the death of her wet nurse, Deborah (Genesis 35:8).

Rachel dies and is buried on the way to Ephrat (Genesis 35:19). By contrast, *nothing* concerning the deaths or burials of Bilhah and Zilpah is recorded in the Biblical narrative. Apparently, these mothers are not buried in the Cave of Machpelah.

Prophecy

Our tradition maintains that the Patriarchs and Matriarchs received many prophecies that are not recorded in the Torah; the Torah describes only a few. One of the prophecies that Jacob received, recorded in the Midrash, was that he would be the progenitor of Twelve Tribes. But he was concerned, because at the age of 84 years (according to Rashi on Genesis 29:21) he had not yet married. Therefore, he said to his uncle Laban: "My days are fulfilled," i.e., "my time is ready, so that the beginning of my prophecy may see fruition." This private prophecy of Jacob's could, on the one hand, serve to strengthen his faith. On the other hand, however, it could create havoc with his personal life if he saw his exclusive function or role as becoming the father of the Twelve Tribes.

Similarly, prophecy may have narrowed the focus of Rachel's and Leah's lives. Rashi states (on Genesis 29:34) that the Matriarchs were prophetesses. The various prophecies that they received -- both recorded and unrecorded in the Torah -- included the information that Jacob would sire twelve sons, who would ultimately become the Twelve Tribes of Israel. This knowledge became central to Rachel's and Leah's relationships with Jacob. They saw their roles and those of Bilhah and Zilpah as facilitating the fulfillment of these prophecies.

When a person focuses *exclusively* on a specific prophecy or thought or idea, the resulting perspective lacks wholeness. One's vision becomes myopic and relationships may become skewed. This may have happened to the Matriarchs. Rather than focusing on the multiple roles of every married woman -- her own identity, wife, mother, lover, etc. -- Rachel and Leah were focused primarily, as were Bilhah and Zilpah, on the role of mother or potential mother. The prophecy about those special twelve children eclipsed and clouded Rachel's and Leah's other, complementary roles of wife and lover in relation to Jacob.

How should a prophecy be interpreted? How should special voices be listened to? The fire of prophecy can become all-consuming and devour the individual. Or, prophecy can illuminate the journey of each individual by enabling the individual to embrace a comprehensive relationship to life, rather than a narrow one.

Rachel and Leah

Jacob's journey, in fulfilling the prophecy that he would sire the Twelve Tribes, is lengthy and complex. The story is well known. He loves Rachel deeply. In fact, he falls in love with her almost at first sight. When Jacob sees Rachel, his first cousin, the daughter of his uncle, Laban, he is so overwhelmed with emotion that he kisses Rachel and cries (Genesis 29:11). Jacob makes an arrangement with Laban whereby Jacob will work for Laban without receiving any wages, but in return, Jacob will be allowed to marry his beloved Rachel. The seven years that he works seem to him as merely a few days, since Jacob's love for Rachel is so intense.

Rachel is described as having a very beautiful appearance and character. Rachel's appearance is captivating, and her presence is enchanting. Rachel has an older sister, whose name is Leah. According to the Midrash (Genesis *Rabbah* 29:16), these sisters are fraternal twins. However, Leah's countenance is strikingly different from that of Rachel. The feature that Jacob notices most about Leah is her eyes. He looks deeply into Leah's eyes, and they appear to him as being *rakkot* (Genesis 29:17), usually translated as "weak." The word "weak" is ambiguous. What does Jacob experience when he looks into Leah's eyes?

The Talmud relates (*Bava Batra* 123a) that since Rebekah had two sons and Laban had two daughters, people thought that the older daughter would marry the older son, and the younger daughter would marry the younger son. Since Rebekah and Laban were sister and brother, it was understood that their children, who were first cousins, would marry one another. Throughout Leah's childhood, she thought that her destiny was to marry Esau, and she cried excessively, both inwardly and outwardly. Her eyes revealed the suffering that she experienced, realizing that her destiny was to marry Esau, who was known to have evil tendencies. The Rabbis interpret Genesis 25:27 as indicating that Esau engaged in idolatry and deceit.

Imagine the impact of this knowledge on Leah's psyche. Marriages frequently took place within extended families, and perhaps there was a custom that the oldest wed the oldest; and the youngest, the youngest. However, were not individual characteristics looked at? Was the entire community gossiping about Leah's fate? Did Leah herself have any choice in the matter? What price did Leah pay for all the years of unnecessary tears and suffering? Did she have trouble sleeping? What were her dreams about? What did she fantasize about? Could she talk to her father or her mother about what people were saying? What communication existed between Leah and her father and her mother? Leah must have had a rather sad childhood, knowing that her marital fate was predetermined. She was denied freedom of choice regarding one of the most important aspects of her life. Her tearful eyes indicated that she was a *prisoner of childhood*.

The seven years of Jacob's servitude to gain the hand of Rachel soon elapsed. At the conclusion of the seven years, Laban made a great feast to celebrate the marriage of Jacob to Rachel. The festivities took place at night, when it was completely dark. The bride was heavily veiled. Jacob was about to fulfill his longed-for hope, his marriage to his beloved Rachel. And then came morning. He felt outraged and deceived when he discovered that Laban had tricked him into marrying Leah.

II

JACOB'S WOUNDED PSYCHE

Jacob and the Birthright

His anguish was threefold. First, his uncle had deceived him. Second, he felt anger towards Leah for her part in the deception. Third, and most importantly, his love for Rachel had turned into torment. Jacob might have wondered: "Could Rachel really have shared our intimate secrets, our secret signs, with her sister Leah so that I could be fooled on my wedding night? Perhaps this ultimate deception is based on my own desire to change my fate. Perhaps by buying the birthright and becoming the firstborn, I was destined to marry Leah, the oldest, and not Rachel."

As twins, Leah and Rachel could represent different, and complementary, aspects of Jacob's personality. The eyes of Leah, which were full of anguish and tears, mirrored Jacob's anguish regarding his betrayal of his brother (Genesis 25:31) and his father (Genesis 27:19). True, he gained the status of firstborn and received the appropriate blessing, but his eyes mirrored inner torment. That part of him was reflected in Leah's eyes.

Jacob also had a public persona. Everyone knew Jacob as a "whole man, dwelling in tents" (Genesis 25:27), giving a beautiful and wholesome appearance to the outside. This positive image is what Jacob saw mirrored in the appearance of his beloved Rachel. On the night of his wedding, Jacob wanted to consummate the relationship between the "whole man, dwelling in tents" and his counterpart, the strikingly beautiful woman. What happened, however, was just the opposite. On a different level, in a different dimension, Jacob the deceiver, the supplanter, was united with a woman who embodied the deception of her father, a woman who had carried pain, suffering and anguish for many years.

The Ladder of Ascension

Jacob was perplexed, because all the above took place in the darkness of the night. Perhaps this darkness caused him to recall an earlier event that also occurred at night -- his dream about the Ladder of Ascension, in which angels of God were ascending and descending. He also heard the voice of God and proclaimed God's Presence, saying "this place is the gate of heaven" (Genesis 28:17). God reconfirmed to Jacob that he would continue in the tradition of his father and grandfather, and all the nations of the world would be blessed through him. The juxtaposition of the numinous event of the Ladder of Ascension with Laban's deception threw Jacob into a state of confusion and intense pain.

Jacob's Anguish

He might have said to himself, at the same time raising his voice to God: "Where are you, God? Cannot the man who is whole and dwells in tents also marry his beloved Rachel? Was the dream of the Ladder of Ascension a hoax, an unlived fantasy? You expressly stated, God, that 'I am with you, and I will watch over you wherever you go' (Genesis 28:15).

Is this how You are with me? Do You not know, God, that Leah is my opposite? What will people think when they look at Leah, with her eyes so tearful? In addition to my love for God and my closeness to the Divine, can I not also experience earthly love with my beloved Rachel?

"Does this mean, O God, that if I had not bought the birthright from my brother, Esau, and if I had remained the second born, then I would have married my beloved Rachel? The image I have of You right now is a God of retribution, Who is exacting revenge. Is it because I supplanted my brother's birthright that You are deceiving me and punishing me by changing brides right before my marriage? I am aware, God, that it is possible for a man to have two wives, one that he loves and one that he loves less.

"You certainly recognized this fact when You wrote a law (Deuteronomy 21:15-17) concerning the determination of who is firstborn when a man has more than one wife. God, You said that the firstborn, even if he is from the less loved wife, still is considered the firstborn, and he shall inherit the family property. He is the *bekhor*. I know, God, what was in Your mind when You wrote this law. You were referring to me and my two wives.

"That law in Deuteronomy is openly painful to me right now. My firstborn is Reuben, the son of Leah, but my true love, my *bekhor* in my heart, is my child of Rachel -- Joseph (Genesis 37:4). O, God, my human experience contradicts Your law. I do not know what to do. Should I rely on my human experience and my feelings, or must I acquiesce and be obedient to a law that is incomprehensible?

The Secret Signs

"How is it possible that I was deceived? Yes, it was dark, yes it was nighttime, yes they were fraternal twins, but I had told my beloved Rachel the secret signs of intimacy that were to be shared by us as bride and bridegroom on our wedding night. It is impossible that Leah would have known these signs, had it not been that my beloved Rachel betrayed me. First, Leah tenderly and passionately touched the great toe of my right foot, then my right thumb, and then my right earlobe (Talmud, *Megillah* 13b).

"The right ear, thumb and toe are also mentioned when Moses consecrated Aaron and his sons as priests (Leviticus (8:23-24). After sacrificing a ram, Moses took from its blood and put it on the right ear, thumb and toe of Aaron, and then went through the same procedure with Aaron's sons. This rite is symbolic. These three parts of the body represent a consecration of the whole body: the ears, to be attentive, and to listen both to what is said and to hear the inner, silent call; the hand, to act; and the foot, to walk in holy ways. Yet, in my case, the touch on these three places was used to deceive me. I was convinced that this was Rachel. No one else knew our signs, other than Rachel and myself. When the sun rose, I discovered, to my shock, that during the night *the voice was the voice of Rachel and the hands were the hands of Leah.*

"I heard the voice of my father saying, 'the voice is the voice of Jacob, and the hands are the hands of Esau' (Genesis 27:22). I felt haunted, and consequently I regretted stealing the blessing from my brother, Esau. I remembered that I was blessed in the "nighttime" of my father's blindness, and I wondered if that deception led to my being deceived in darkness as well. I felt scared that this theft would stay with me all the days of my life, and I would eternally be known as Jacob, the Betrayer. When I would walk with my wife, and people would see Leah, everyone would take note that my deceitful past molded my unhappy future.

"Those secret signs of the foot, the thumb and the ear symbolized a loving connection between body and soul. When I was touched on my foot, thumb and ear, I thought I felt Rachel's soul. But the morning showed otherwise. It was merely a physical touch on my foot, thumb and ear, without the inner loving connection to the soul. Body and soul became dichotomous. My desire for a complete union grew even more. And my uncle said, almost flippantly, 'in another seven days, you can have Rachel as your beloved wife, and then work for another seven years.'"

Rachel was torn between trying to prevent her sister's embarrassment on Leah's first night together with Jacob, and honoring her loving relationship and loyalty to Jacob. Presumably, she may have thought as follows: "I love Jacob dearly, and I certainly would not want to lose him as a husband-to-be, nor do I want to lose his love. I also do not want to deceive him. But at the same time, I do not want my sister to be shamed and humiliated. I cannot win, for there are opposing emotions within me --

those concerning my sister and those revolving around my husband-to-be. For right now, I am deciding to protect my twin sister, for she represents my other half and my family of origin, and she and I have been together for so many years. My potential family life with Jacob is something that lies in the future, although even now, he is my beloved."

In the stillness and darkness of the night, as Leah was taking Rachel's place at the entrance to Jacob's tent, Rachel whispered to her sister the secret touches that Jacob and Rachel had previously devised as a sign known only to them (Talmud, *Megillah* 13b).

Barrenness and Fertility

Jacob loved Rachel immensely. When they were finally allowed to wed, Jacob's desire for closeness and intimacy, sexuality and sensuality was fulfilled with his beloved Rachel in a way that it had not been with Leah (Genesis 29:30). Jacob's love for Rachel was based not only on physical attraction, but also on his recognition of her spiritual qualities. God saw all this, and He was displeased that Jacob did not love Leah. The omnipotent God said: "I will create a situation where Jacob will be forced to love his wives as equally as possible." His beloved wife, Rachel, became barren, and his less loved Leah conceived. So now, his firstborn was not from his beloved Rachel, but from his less beloved Leah. He, who had bought the birthright to become the firstborn in his family, now was given a firstborn from a wife that he did not love wholeheartedly.

"Does God create barrenness and infertility as a manipulatory device and an intervention to enhance marital happiness? Naturally, when one has a child, one feels more whole and presumably, more content. However, a parental role does not necessarily have a beneficial effect on the marital relationship. Right at the beginning of Creation and after the Flood during the time of Noah, God emphasized the beauty of 'to be fruitful and multiply' (Genesis 1:28). I listened to God's words, 'be fruitful and multiply,' yet I experienced God's actions. First, He arranged for me to marry Leah, and then He caused my beloved Rachel to become infertile."

Does a man love his wife more if she bears him children? Is barrenness a wife's responsibility exclusively? If a man has children, he assumes the new role of a father. A man's love for his wife is a spousal relationship, not a parental relationship. Having children is, obviously, certainly a blessing, but it does not alter the spousal care, commitment, intimacy and love for one another. Yet, does God think otherwise? It is hard for me to imagine that God intervenes regarding childbearing, to enhance Jacob's love for Leah. Children are not a means, but their existence is a blessing in itself. I apologize for saying this, but God presents Himself in a puzzling manner in the role of marriage counselor.

Rachel's Jealousy

Leah and Jacob give birth to four children: Reuben, Simeon, Levi and Judah. God, do You think that this alleviates the plight of Leah? Do You think, do You really think that Jacob loves her more now? Are You not aware that there is spousal love and there is parental love, and they are not identical, nor do they supplant one another? If anything, God, Leah feels more isolated and lonely. Not only does Jacob still prefer Rachel over Leah, but now Rachel has become envious of Leah. In the midst of her jealousy, Rachel makes a most startling statement: "O, Jacob, give me children, or else I would rather be dead!" Rachel is jealous of her sister. Her envy grows after Leah gives birth to four sons, and Rachel is still barren. The Midrash says that Rachel is not only jealous, but she feels that Leah is more righteous than she. She reasons that were Leah not more righteous, she would not merit giving birth to *banim*, translated either as "sons," referring to her first four sons, or "children," (Genesis *Rabbah* 30:1). This Midrash seems to imply that through Leah's righteousness, she merited having children, or specifically, sons.

I am concerned that infertile couples who read this Midrash might understand their childlessness as Rachel did, thinking it indicates a lack of righteousness on their part.

Ultimately, we must come to the realization that childlessness, like illnesses or other afflictions that confront us, can serve as points of departure for exploration of the mysteries of our lives and existence.

Barrenness and Death

The Midrash continues by interpreting Rachel's statement that unless she can have children, she will be considered as a dead person. This statement may be understood *metaphorically* as Rachel's expressing a very strong desire to have children.

To support this interpretation, I offer a recurrent clinical example from my pastoral rounds. Almost daily, a patient who is experiencing excruciating pain will proclaim: "I want to die." Though some people may indeed harbor a death wish (*thanatos*), what most of these patients are expressing is that they would like the pain to be alleviated, not that they want death to come immediately.

I vividly recall my very first visit at Cedars-Sinai on August 7, 1978 at 11:00 a.m. My beeper went off, and the first professional call I had as Chaplain took me to a terminally ill patient in the Special Care Unit on the sixth floor, room 6815. She asked me to recite the *Viddui* (a confessional prayer) with her, as she felt her death was imminent. After conversing with her, I began to recite the *Viddui* with her, in Hebrew and in English. When she saw the seriousness of the moment and envisioned the Angel of Death coming to take her, she turned to me and said: "Excuse me, Rabbi Meier, I want to bake another cake for my grandchildren before I die." It became clear that she was not really ready to recite the *Viddui* or to die.

Similarly, with regard to Rachel, her expression that likens barrenness to death is really a deeper expression of her strong desire for children. Unfortunately, Rachel's statement has been misunderstood and has caused misery and anguish to people who have not been able to have children.

What exactly does the desire to have children mean? This complex desire obviously means different things to different people. First, it allows one to create life itself. Giving birth and creating another life means taking on an essential aspect of God. The first act that God demonstrates in the Torah is creation (Genesis 1:1). When we create life, and when we give birth, this is an ultimate fulfillment of walking in the ways of God.

Second, everyone struggles with his or her own mortality and search for meaning in this temporal life. When our life is continued through our progeny, whom we create, we have a feeling of going beyond the finite and achieving immortality. Perhaps Rachel's statement, in which she equates childlessness with death, reflects her observation that without children, one's own line dies out.

Third, the desire to have children also reflects the remarkable truth that despite the struggles of life, and despite the immense pain and suffering in the world, people maintain hope and faith in the future of humanity.

Although these three possible understandings of the desire to have children reflect lofty thoughts, I suggest that life has enormous meaning, even without the creation of new human life. It would be absurd to think that the meaning of life is *exclusively* to continue life, as Viktor Frankl (1984) observed: "Procreation is not the only meaning of life, for then life in itself would become meaningless, and something that in itself is meaningless cannot be rendered meaningful merely by its perpetuation." The experience of life must have some value in and of itself. Unfortunately, Rachel fails to recognize this truth.

The Value of Life

Rachel's humanness is revealed as she proclaims from the honest depth of her soul that life for a woman is worthless without progeny. As she confronts Jacob, does she really think that he is responsible for her barrenness? Or, by confronting her husband, is she acting out her anger?

If the only thing that Rachel wants to continue is life in the form of children, then she overlooks the fact that her own life also has value. Perhaps what Rachel is expressing is her anger at her plight. After all, she is a beautiful woman, both externally and internally. She has been pursued by her beloved Jacob. She is well known for her hospitality. Yet, she is unable to have children. Is barrenness a punishment? Is barrenness an illness? "What have I done to deserve this? Inwardly, I compare myself to my sister. She has stolen my husband, granted with my reluctant assistance. I cannot even look into my sister's eyes. She cried, she cried and she still cries, and yet *I* am barren. What an absurdity. Did God, perhaps, want me to be discontented all my life?"

Jacob's Response to Rachel's Infertility

Jacob is bewildered. It is hard for him to comprehend the words and anger of his beloved Rachel. Is this the same Rachel who is so beautiful? And he responds: "I am not in place of God," (Genesis 30:2), implying that fertility is exclusively dependent upon the blessing of God.

Jacob and Rachel's dialogue regarding her inability to bear children reflects deep marital conflict, as each partner points a finger at the other in an angry manner. In response to Rachel's plea to bear children, Jacob states (according to Rashi on Genesis 30:2) that *he* has children, namely from Leah, but Rachel does not. It is God who has withheld children from Rachel. I think this was one of the most painful responses that Jacob could choose. (The *Siftey Hakhamim*, in his commentary on this verse, also points out that Jacob, as a righteous person, should have responded in a gentle manner.) Does he want to emphasize his blessings, and thereby accentuate her agony at being barren? Is this the Rachel whom he loves, and whose appearance is so beautiful and captivating? How can he cause her hurt and pain? One possible interpretation is to view Jacob's words as an educational and corrective response. He wants to make clear to his wife that fertility and procreation are, ultimately, not controlled by humans, but by God.

Rachel's Selection of Bilhah

Upon hearing Jacob's words, which feel non-comforting and defensive, Rachel's anger intensifies. She decides to share her female attendant, Bilhah, with her husband, so that the child of that union can become her child as well.

How does Rachel feel as she shares her female attendant, Bilhah, with her husband? Certainly, the mores of Biblical times included polygamy and concubinage. However, it is hard to believe that there was no intimate emotion at all involved in these sexual relationships. Perhaps Rachel is speechless, and that is why the sentence that describes this arrangement is so terse (Genesis 30:4 contains only 9 Hebrew words). But Rachel's thoughts may include jealousy, anger, regret, hurt and confusion, as she suffers in silence.

Another interpretation of Rachel's thought processes might imagine her inner dialogue as follows: "First, I give Leah and now I give Bilhah. Is Jacob my husband, or everyone else's husband? What does my husband think when he is with me? Does he know it is me? Or, does he think I am Leah or Bilhah? After all, both Leah and I touch Jacob sensually in exactly the same three places.

"Will this further alienate Jacob from me? I am his beloved, but he had four children with Leah, and now, presumably, he may have children with Bilhah. Where will that put me? Will these children be Bilhah's, mine or both of ours? Who will nurse the children? Will I be able to nurse the children? Whom will they call 'Mommy?' Will I be a stepmother, or will I become their mother? I do not want to denigrate Bilhah. I remember how Sarah, my grandmother by marriage, afflicted Hagar, after she and Abraham gave birth to Ishmael. I want to respect Bilhah, yet I want to raise the child. How can I do this to another woman, particularly my female attendant? Am I using Bilhah's body and discarding her soul? I am in torment. Jacob wants children from me. I am jealous of my sister, Leah, and I am taking advantage of Bilhah's body. How will this child be mine?"

Leah and Zilpah

Jacob and Bilhah gave birth to two children, Dan and Naftali. Meanwhile, Leah ceased bearing children. She said to herself: "If Rachel can give Bilhah to Jacob, I can give my female attendant, Zilpah, to Jacob as well." So Jacob and Zilpah gave birth to two children, Gad and Asher.

How can one explain Leah's reaction to her inability to continue bearing children? She and Jacob gave birth to four sons. Her oldest is even considered the firstborn to Jacob. Yet now, she still feels inadequate. Is the purpose of any woman in a marital relationship primarily or exclusively to bear children? Is that why she gave Zilpah to Jacob -- to bear children -- so that Jacob's prophecy regarding his siring the Twelve Tribes of Israel would be fulfilled?

I can only speculate about the relationship of a woman to her female attendant. "Is this a female attendant, or is this my husband's concubine? A female attendant is dear to me, but I am jealous of my husband's concubine. I know that I have taken my female attendant and transformed her into my husband's concubine. Please understand that this came about as a result of my feeling femininely inadequate, not being able to bear more children. I do not like to own another person, and I certainly feel very uncomfortable in dictating another woman's sexual pleasures with my husband. This is beyond what I can comprehend, yet this is the social milieu and culture in which I live.

"Sometimes, I haphazardly accept the mores of our times, but at other times, I seriously question these values. I know that these values are lived by the great people of our time, including Abraham, my grandfather by marriage. Nevertheless, the experience of my life leads me to feel and think otherwise. I cannot arbitrarily use another woman's body to fulfill my inadequacy. Excuse me for asking this most tender question, but should not the conception of children be the result of warmth, love, intimacy and spiritual union, and not merely the biological union of two people?

"So take a look at us two sisters, Rachel and Leah. Both of us, at one point in our lives, seem to be unable to bear children. We provide our mutual husband with our female attendants to serve as his concubines. Please note that ultimately, we are two of the Matriarchs of the entire Jewish people. And we also have the audacity, naturally according to the mores of our times, to exclude Bilhah and Zilpah from the prestigious Matriarchs. Why are we excluding them? If we raise their children, which obviously causes them maternal anguish, do we have to cause them further pain by banishing them completely from being Matriarchs? Why, oh why, is there so much exclusion of the other? The feelings of superiority that lead to exclusion usually reflect inner feelings of inadequacy. Am I so inadequate? Are we so inadequate?"

Jacob's Four Women

Jacob, the "whole person, dwelling in tents," now has four different women visiting his tent. He definitely has ambivalent feelings. He wonders why Rachel and Leah have so willingly shared Bilhah and Zilpah. "I love my two wives, independent of their childbearing capacity. As a matter of fact, I am obsessed with Rachel, and she occupies my thoughts, my feelings and my raison d'etre. She is my beloved wife. Yet now, I also love Leah. When our third child, Levi, was born, I selected his name, because I felt then that through his birth we were united. If you want to know the truth, my truth, I did not know what to do when Bilhah and Zilpah visited my tent to be with me. I knew they had received consent from Rachel and Leah, but Rachel is my beloved regardless, and I learned to love Leah as well. Were Bilhah and Zilpah meant as an additional satisfaction for my sexual desire, for procreation or just for confusion? Is this the way my children, the future Twelve Tribes of Israel, are conceived?

"O, God, I remember what You told me in my dream of the Ladder of Ascension, that my offspring will be as many as the dust of the earth and shall spread west, east, north and south, and that eventually, all the nations shall be blessed through them, my children. But God, I do not want such multitudes of children if it will create unhappiness and jealousy for Rachel and Leah. So far, I have eight children, eight beautiful children, but my very beloved wife, Rachel, is still barren. Perhaps, God, You have a master plan that presumably I am not privy to, but are we all pawns in the evolution of the destiny and fate of the Jewish people and humanity? Do not forget, I am Jacob, 'a whole person, dwelling in tents,' and I focus also on the here-and-now. The present obviously leads into the future, but the experience of the present must also be comprehensible, no matter what role it is to play in a Divine master plan. Life is not meaningful because of tomorrow, but because of today. And I do not experience that.

Jacob's Sabbath Table

"God, let me share with You a Friday-night *Shabbat* meal in my tent, as I experience it. It begins with my four wives lighting candles, yet the light brings darkness, and the *Shabbat* Queen brings jealousy. I love to sing the *Eshet Hayil* ('Woman of Valor') song, which I sing only once. Paradoxically, when I come to the phrase, 'and you surpass them all,' I have all four women in mind, but specifically Rachel. The four women would prefer that I sing this song four times, but each one wants it sung to her first. All eight children call me *Abba*, father, in a reverential manner, but when they call *Ima* ('Mommy'), Rachel responds for Bilhah, and Leah responds for Zilpah. We sing songs at the *Shabbat* table, but Bilhah and Zilpah sit silently and do not participate in our singing. Their silence torments me. I hear their silent cries, the pain of their hearts. What disturbs me most is the quiet conversation that ensues between my four wives. I do not know what they are saying, but I feel very uncomfortable.

I think I have secrets with each one of them, but when I see all four communicating quietly, I begin to wonder whether all four share secrets about me.

"Right before the *kiddush*, I bless my children with great devotion and piety. I ask God to be with each one of them. Naturally, I bless Reuben first. He is my *bekhor* (firstborn), but so is Dan to Bilhah and Gad to Zilpah. During all this time, Rachel cries internally. Sibling rivalry is rampant, as each child awaits his turn for the parental blessing. O, God, this is my *Shabbat* table: jealousy, sibling rivalry, tears, barrenness, secrets, whispering and silence."

Reuben and the Mandrakes

Leah temporarily ceases bearing children. Seeing this, her son Reuben, the firstborn to Jacob, assumes a leadership role. He brings *duda'im* (mandrakes - a fruit-bearing plant) to his mother, Leah. These love-flowers are understood to be aphrodisiacs, i.e., substances that excite sexual desire. Reuben hopes to create an atmosphere in which his parents will continue to engage in sexual relations, so that his mother will continue to bear children. He further hopes that the children of this union, Reuben's full siblings, will transform Leah into a more beloved wife. Apparently, once Leah ceased giving birth, Jacob's attention was focused on Zilpah.

I am confused. In Jacob's mind, what is the relationship between loving his wife Leah and her inability to bear children? Even if Leah is not as beloved as Rachel, is it possible that after having four children with Leah, Jacob finds that his love, caring and sensitivity for her have become diminished? Did Reuben sense this and want to modify the situation?

Furthermore, what is an aphrodisiac? How does a love-flower stimulate sexual desire? The fragrance is captivating, and the fruit itself may raise the level of sexual arousal. Yet, who is being aroused? Is Leah being aroused by the special fragrance and by a new level of sexual desire? Is Jacob being aroused by this new atmosphere surrounding Leah?

Should not real sexual desire between man and woman, between husband and wife, be dependent upon a soul connection? Is not this special intimate union part of the undefinable, mystical and mysterious side of the human spirit? Is not sexuality the marriage of anima and animus, of heaven and earth? Is not the real aphrodisiac one that needs to be developed and nurtured through shared experiences, feelings and intimate thoughts?

Upon seeing Leah receive the mandrakes from Reuben, Rachel, the completely barren wife, politely implores Leah to share some of the mandrakes with her. Rachel reasons that even if Leah has temporarily ceased bearing children, Leah already has four children, compared to Rachel's own life of complete barrenness, tears and jealousy.

Leah responds to her sister and co-wife, Rachel, stating that this is unbelievably unfair. "Recognizing that you have Jacob's special affection, you also now want to take a special aphrodisiac from my son?" Apparently, Leah's sadness has reached new depths, in her realization that bearing four children, and raising them, has not yet endeared her to Jacob.

A Woman's Roles

Leah's statement and her anguish indicate that she confuses the role of woman as mother, a maternal function, with that of woman as wife, a spousal relationship. Completely different feminine qualities are involved in each of these functions. The central aspect of a maternal function is the Great Mother, who nurtures and nourishes throughout life, while the essence of a loving spousal relationship focuses more on the feminine soul-like qualities or anima. These two feminine aspects are not mutually exclusive; they co-exist, each with varying degrees of dominance, at any given time.

As a result of this dichotomy, Rachel strikes a bargain with her rival, Leah. She enables Leah to be intimate with Jacob on that night; in exchange, Rachel receives aphrodisiacs from Reuben. This arrangement is seen by our Rabbis as degrading the sanctity of the marital relationship. Rachel did not demonstrate adequate respect for the sexual intimacy of her husband, Jacob. The Rabbis state that consequently, she did not merit to be buried with him (Talmud, *Niddah* 31). She was buried where she died, on the way to Ephrat, not in the Cave of Machpelah.

Additionally, this episode makes it seem almost as if Rachel's barrenness and anguish would cause her to act without limits in an attempt to bear children. When Jacob returns home that evening, Leah runs out to meet him and says to her husband: "You will come to me, because I have hired you with my son's mandrakes" (Genesis 30:16). It is difficult to understand the psyches of Rachel and Leah in relationship to their common husband, Jacob. Obviously, they each desire him -- Rachel, out of her love and to bear him children; and Leah, to become more beloved and to continue to bear children also. Obviously, they both want children. Nevertheless, neither of them appears to be particularly pious or modest in her endeavors. The word "hire" has a connotation that spousal intimacy takes the form of prostitution. In this case, it is not the man who pays, but Rachel and Leah who agree to some bargain with each other so that Leah may sleep with Jacob.

God hears the voice of Leah, and she gives birth to Issachar, Zebulun and Dinah. Is there not a difference between sexual desire and fertility? It seems that both Rachel and Leah, and certainly Reuben, think that the arousal of sexual desire is the cause of procreation. However, Jacob thinks differently. He tells Rachel that fertility is in the hands of God (Genesis 30:2). Here we have two completely different understandings of childbearing. Jacob believes that the birth of all children is sacred, the result of a union between man, woman and God. Leah and Rachel seem to feel that Jacob's abstinence from sexual intimacy is due to their infertility, as if his love for his wives is dependent upon their ability to bear children.

Rachel's Children

After Leah has six sons and one daughter, God remembers Rachel. Rachel and Jacob have a child, whom they call Joseph. Nothing is indicated in the text as to why God remembers Rachel at this time. Later on, Rachel gives birth to one more child, and her labor is very difficult. During the labor process, the midwife says to her: "Do not be afraid. This shall also be a son" (Genesis 35:17). Rachel understands this to be a fulfillment of the name of her first son, Joseph, which means that God will give her an additional son. During the difficult labor process, Rachel's dying process begins. As she gives birth, she calls out that the name of this child should be *Ben Oni*, "the son of my sorrow." However, Jacob calls the son Benjamin, translated as either "the son of my right hand," or "the son of my old age." Rachel is buried on the way to Ephrat, near

Bethlehem. A monument at her burial place is still in existence. How sad and ironic it is that Rachel, who longs for children her entire life, dies in childbirth.

Rachel's Weeping

The Torah's last description of Rachel vividly portrays her painful labor preceding her death: "...And Rachel travailed, and she had hard labor..." (Genesis 35:16-18). One can imagine that during this difficult process, Rachel was crying and wailing. Somehow, the tears that began during that birthing process, which was also Rachel's dying process, never stopped.

Rachel is depicted for all time as weeping over her children, who have been sent into exile, waiting for their ingathering: "...A voice is heard in Ramah, groaning, weeping, and bitter lamentation; Rachel is weeping for her children; she refuses to be comforted for her children because they are not (here)..." (Jeremiah 31:14-16). This picture of a tearful Rachel is ironic, since it was a tearful Leah who caused the young Jacob to prefer the beautiful and content Rachel over her twin sister. Sometimes those elements of life that we once successfully evade seem fated to confront us again at a later date.

Now it is Rachel who weeps. However, the tears of Rachel are different from those of Leah. Leah was tearful because her freedom was circumscribed; others had determined that she would marry Esau. Rachel's tears continue to be shed until the time of the promised redemption and Ingathering of the Exiles. All of Rachel's children will then return to Israel. Until that time, Rachel mourns the loss of national, rather than personal freedom and self-determination.

It is an irony of history that Jacob's beloved Rachel not only is transformed into a tearful woman, like Leah, but also is fated to continue crying until the ultimate redemption of her children.

III

THE STRUGGLE

The Biblical Nomenclature for Jacob's Wives

How does the Torah refer to Rachel, Leah, Bilhah and Zilpah? In most places, Rachel and Leah are each called Jacob's "wife." In most places (e.g., Genesis 29:24, 33:1, 35:25, 26), Bilhah and Zilpah are referred to as *shefahot*, "female attendants" or "handmaidens." In one place, Bilhah is called a *pilegesh*, "concubine" (Genesis 35:22).

However, there is a singular Biblical verse that is striking in its reference to Bilhah and Zilpah. In Genesis 37:2, they are called his "wives." That verse refers to the seventeen-year-old Joseph, who "was feeding the flock with his brethren, and he was a lad, even with the sons of Bilhah, and with the sons of Zilpah, his father's wives..." Even when something occurs only once in the Biblical text, it is significant. For example, the central principle of belief that "the Lord is One" is found only once (Deuteronomy 6:4).

Bilhah and Zilpah are also referred to individually as Jacob's *isha* (Genesis 30:4, 9), but these references must be understood in their contexts. In these verses, *isha* should be understood as "woman," not "wife." Immediately after these verses, reference is made to Bilhah's and Zilpah's conceiving or giving birth to a child. Thus, the term *isha* appears to define the function, and not the status of Bilhah and Zilpah. Indeed, in those same verses, the women are each defined as a *shifhah*. Subsequently, when Bilhah and Zilpah give birth, Rachel and Leah select the names for the children of the *shefahot*, illustrating that they regard the children as their own offspring.

The one reference to Bilhah and Zilpah as wives occurs after the deaths of Rachel and Leah. It is possible that even though the women are accorded spousal status at this late point, the terminology of "wives" indicates Jacob's inner torment over a long period. One can imagine how Jacob may have felt throughout the years he lived with all four women. He lived intimately with Bilhah and Zilpah and sired four sons with them, fulfilling part of his prophetic vision that he would father Twelve Tribes. I think that Jacob would have wanted Bilhah and Zilpah to be granted the status of wives and Matriarchs. His emotions must have been torn as he heard the constant references to Bilhah and Zilpah as female attendants. Finally, after the death of Rachel and Leah, the other women in his life could be called "wives."

As a hospital chaplain and psychologist who has counseled many clients, I have seen a recurring pattern among people who remarry in their later years, after the death of a spouse. Often, these individuals tell me that they fantasized about marrying someone else for a long time, even during the years that they were happily married.

Perhaps the category of *shifhah*, "female attendant," includes women who are fantasized about, but who are not yet attainable. If this is the case, it could account for Jacob's inner torment throughout his lifetime, which he alludes to when he meets the Egyptian Pharaoh. Although Bilhah and Zilpah have by then been granted the status of wives, Jacob's years of inner agony seems to have taken their toll, and his pain remains.

The Days of Jacob's Life

When Joseph presented his family to the Pharaoh, the Egyptian ruler asked Jacob how old he was. Jacob responded: "The days of the years of my sojournings [are] a hundred and thirty years..." (Genesis 47:9). He could have stopped there, yet he continued, saying "few and evil have been the days of the years of my life...," indicating that his life had been basically unhappy.

During Jacob's life, he was confronted by a number of external threats and challenges which were resolved in his favor. Yet, his own internal struggles caused him to make a subjective judgment, at the age of 130, that "few and evil have been the days of the years of my life." He further observed that "[the days of my life] have not attained [unto] the days of the years of the life of my fathers in the days of their sojournings" (Genesis 47:9). Jacob's father, Isaac, lived to 180, and his grandfather, Abraham, lived to the age of 175, so that Jacob's reference to his life span, in comparison to theirs, can be easily understood.

Rashi comments on this verse that Jacob's comparison is made "in respect to happiness." One simple explanation of Jacob's self-assessment is that the "evil" that befell him refers to external events. He had conflict from early on with his brother Esau. He was deceived by his father-in-law, Laban. He confronted the barrenness of his beloved Rachel. He experienced immeasurable agony, thinking that his beloved son, Joseph, was dead. For some twenty years, he mourned this loss. Finally, in old age, he and his family faced famine in their homeland, and his sons experienced arduous travels and encounters in Egypt.

All these events can certainly justify the response of "few and evil have been the days of the years of my life." However, another interpretation is possible. Jacob seems to have faced an inner conflict in dealing with the four women in his life -- two "wives" and two "female attendants" initially; and later, two "wives" who had once been called *shefahot*.

Jacob was put to a test at a crucial point in his life, and this experience exacerbated his inner conflict. Before he encountered Esau for the first time since he had left home, Jacob divided his household into three camps. Genesis 33:2 recounts the order of the encampment. He put himself first, "and he put the handmaids and their children foremost, and Leah and her children after, and Rachel and Joseph hindermost."

At the time that he decided on this order of march, Jacob's internal struggle became externalized. He had to think about who might die first and who would be saved in the event of a bloody encounter with Esau. His public persona, "a whole man, dwelling in tents," mandated that he think of a wife as a wife, and a female attendant as a female attendant in considering where to place them and their children. Furthermore, in thinking about his relationship with his wives, Jacob could not help but be reminded of his first wedding, years before, when he wanted his beloved Rachel but was tricked into marrying Leah.

Jacob's choice of camp order seems ironic in light of all that transpired afterwards. Although Joseph was put at the rear, to ensure his protection and survival, it was he who was later wrenched from his father's house, presumed dead and mourned by Jacob.

Jacob's internal and external conflict regarding his wives may well explain his response of "few and evil have been the days of the years of my life." When he was young, he was tricked into marrying Leah, whom he did not want at that point in his life. She always remained his less beloved wife. Jacob's beloved wife, Rachel, died in childbirth, and he never fully recovered from that loss. Every time that he gazed upon Joseph's handsome face, he was reminded of Joseph's mother, the beautiful Rachel. Near the end of Jacob's life, he interjected a reference to Rachel's death while he was speaking to Joseph: "...Rachel died unto me in the land of Canaan in the way, when [there was] still some way to come unto Ephrat; and I buried her there in the way to Ephrat..." (Genesis 48:7).

Furthermore, for much of his life Jacob lived with four women, two of them called *shefahot*, all of whom bore him the sons who became the Twelve Tribes. The role of the *shefahot* is unclear, since the Torah also calls them "wives."

The Rabbis were aware of Jacob's conflict concerning the roles of the women in his life. Although they generally refer to four Matriarchs (e.g., Talmud *Berakhot* 16b speaks of Sarah, Rebekah, Rachel and Leah), there is one Rabbinic reference to *six* Matriarchs. In the Midrash, Numbers *Rabbah*, Chapter 12, *Piska* 17, the Rabbis refer to the six Matriarchs, including Bilhah and Zilpah.

It is interesting that Jacob's inner torment resonated within the Sages as they wrestled with the status of Bilhah and Zilpah, mothers of four of the Tribes of Israel.

Jacob's Illness

Near the end of Jacob's life, the Torah refers to the fact that Jacob became sick. He is the first person in the Torah so described. Prior to Jacob, people continued to feel well throughout the years of their lives, and then they died.

However, Genesis 48:1 states: "And it came to pass after these things, that one said to Joseph: 'Behold, thy father is sick'...," causing Joseph to go visit the ailing Jacob. I think that in this verse, the Torah hints at the etiology of illness, suggesting it is precipitated by inner conflict such as that experienced by Jacob.

When one lives with inner conflict all the days of his life and at the age of 130 says "few and evil have been the days of the years of my life," his torment may subsequently express itself in some visible illness. Jacob ultimately lived to 147 years of age. His self-awareness and painful assessment of his inner conflicts may have occupied much of his life. Despite Jacob's internal torment regarding the roles of his wives, no Tribe is regarded as superior based on which son of Jacob was born to which mother; all of the Twelve Tribes are viewed as equals.

Jacob's Beloved Rachel

As pointed out previously, Jacob did not accede to Rachel's dying wish regarding the naming of their second son. Instead of calling him *Ben Oni*, "the son of my sorrow," Jacob called their son Benjamin, meaning either "the son of my right hand," or "the son of my old age."

Jacob wanted fond memories of Rachel. He did not want to remember her always with sorrow, but rather with positive images. One can maintain love for a person who is no longer present. Jacob wanted Rachel to remain his beloved even after her death, so he tried to hold on to a mental image of her smiling. However, Providence intervened, and Jacob was left with a vision of a tearful, crying Rachel.

Jacob learned a difficult lesson, one that we must absorb as well. He first rejected the teary-eyed Leah, making some negative assumptions about people who experience inner sorrow. However, people who have suffered are indeed capable of proceeding with their inner life journey; they are not doomed to remain always in tears.

When Jacob saw Leah in tears, he should not have assumed that he would have a terrible life if he married her. He could have thought: "This is a woman who has tasted suffering, but she will grow beyond it." Instead, Jacob pursued and wed Rachel who, ironically, has become the tearful Matriarch for the ages.

Jacob might have chosen not to call his youngest son *Ben Oni* so as not to burden the boy with a negative, guilt-ridden name that might haunt the child throughout his life. However, it seems clear that he also changed his son's name to Benjamin in order to project and protect a positive image of Rachel and himself. Jacob did not carry out Rachel's deathbed request due to overriding considerations. Who knows how Rachel would be remembered if her son had, in fact, been named *Ben Oni*?

Shared Qualities

To Jacob, the trick played on him at his first wedding -- when Leah was switched with her twin sister, Rachel -- was pivotal. When he found that Leah was his wife, he felt deceived and betrayed, saddled with a tearful woman whose problems he did not want to share. Jacob should have realized that even if he had wed only Rachel, he would have married a part of Leah -- the Leah qualities, such as crying, tearfulness and sadness.

Ordinarily, under the marriage canopy, a form of magic takes place. The bride and groom change, yet are not even aware of this transformation. A man becomes a husband and potential father. A woman becomes a wife and potential mother. In addition to the positive qualities of each partner, the shadow or negative aspects of both individuals are joined. During our lives, we inherit and sometimes adopt some attributes and projections of our fathers, mothers, twins and other siblings. Thus, by marrying only Rachel, Jacob would have still confronted some aspects of Leah. The deception that Jacob experienced happens to everyone at some point in his or her life.

IV

HEALING

God's Presence

When Jacob dreamt about the Ladder of Ascension, God's central promise to him was "I am with you" (Genesis 28:12-15). A human being cannot ask for anything more than this greatest of all blessings.

Jacob understood and appreciated this Divine gift. He was a man who deeply and analytically examined all aspects of his life, including his dreams. He lived a rich and meaningful life, confronting both his conscious and unconscious experiences, encounters and needs.

What remains is a somewhat contradictory and paradoxical portrait of Jacob. On the one hand, his public persona was the "whole man, dwelling in tents." On the other hand, by his own assessment, the internal, subjective Jacob was someone who felt that "few and evil have been the days of the years of my life."

The last sentence of the Book of Micah (7:20) can perhaps clarify the nature of Jacob's internal conflicts, as well as his legacy. The Prophet states that "You [God] will give *truth* to Jacob..." Rashi comments that this promise echoes what Jacob was told in his dream at the Ladder of Ascension: "*And behold, I am with thee...for I will not leave thee*" (Genesis 28:15). Rashi points out that what "You promised in truth to Jacob" will be given also to his *descendants*.

What is truth? One view is that it is a subjective concept, based on where a human being is at a particular point in his or her life. An individual's concept of different "truths" changes over time. For example, one's acceptance of different, personal images of God at different states of life is part of normal psychological and religious development.

Whatever a person's human, subjective "truth" is, the individual should ideally find accord and harmony between the internal and the external life. There should be no disparity between belief and action. Where such disparity exists, one should at least try to be consciously aware of it. Real truth may mean that the subjective psyche and the external self mesh perfectly.

Jacob certainly felt that God was with him. Therefore, his self-assessment that "few and evil have been the days of the years of my life" needs to be understood in context. It was made to the powerful Egyptian Pharaoh, ruler of his country, under whose shelter Jacob and his children had come to seek sustenance and protection. Rather than stress the strengths of himself and his family, Jacob may have prudently chosen to stress the vulnerable and weak aspects of his clan. He wanted to ensure governmental protection for himself, Joseph and the rest of his progeny, and his response to the Pharaoh was sure to elicit a caring and sensitive reaction.

The word "days" in Jacob's response to the Pharaoh is particularly significant. "Days" represent one's conscious thoughts and actions. At those times, Jacob may have felt alone, beset by conflict and grappling with challenges. But during the *night* hours, while confronting his unconscious and the deepest recesses of his psyche, Jacob always knew that God was with him. The promise that God would always be with him was made to him at *night*, during the dream of the Ladder of Ascension. Similarly, though Jacob was alone at *night* when he struggled with the angel or *Ish*, and that confrontation continued until the dawn of the new day, Jacob's response was "I was privileged to see God face to face" (Genesis 32:25-33).

Even when we confront external challenges that make us feel totally alone, we can recognize that God is with us. The following tale by an unknown author illustrates how God's Presence can be experienced even during times of trial and tribulation.

FOOTPRINTS

One night a man dreamt that he was walking along the beach with God. Across the sky flashed scenes from his life. For each scene, he noticed two sets of footprints in the sand: one belonging to him, and the other to God.

He looked back at the footprints in the sand. He noticed that many times along the path of his life there was only one set of footprints. He also noticed that this happened at the very lowest and saddest times in his life.

This really bothered him and he questioned God about it: "You said that You would walk with me all the way. But during some of the most troublesome times in my life, there is only one set of footprints. I don't understand why when I needed You most, You would leave me."

God replied: "My precious, precious child, I love you and I would never leave you. During your times of trial and suffering, when you see only one set of footprints, it was then that I carried you."

An Assessment of Jacob's Life and Legacy

Jacob's continuing struggles during his lifetime are representative of the human predicament. Human beings continue to struggle with internal and external conflict and challenges. Many of Jacob's most significant challenges can be understood as prototypical of situations that confront almost everyone at one time or another. The following examples illustrate how we all share many of Jacob's experiences:

1. Jacob's problems with his brother, *Esau*, are representative of *sibling rivalry*. Most families with more than one child experience tensions and rivalries as each child strives for a favored position in the family constellation. Such rivalry exists in varying degrees in most households, although the nature and severity of the problem change over the years. This age-old aspect of family life is part of the human condition.

2. Similarly, Jacob's relationship with *Laban* is representative of the issues that arise between married individuals and their *in-laws*. When two families merge, it is inevitable that different backgrounds, perspectives and understandings create potential or actual conflict. The acknowledgment of these family dynamics is the first step in resolving many disagreements.

3. Jacob's *four wives* help us understand the nature of *the real and the ideal spouse* in a marriage relationship. A husband has a real wife, but he may also fantasize about an ideal anima (female) figure. Likewise, a wife may fantasize about an ideal animus (male) figure. We all have fantasy figures, who are real and significant in that they exist in the psyche. Acknowledging them can enrich a marriage, rather than threaten it.

4. Jacob experienced a period of *famine*, which forced him and his family to relocate to Egypt. The modern family is also faced with *financial problems* and times of economic distress, when the family's very survival is at stake.

5. Isaac and Rebekah's parenting of *Jacob and Esau* makes one think of *enmeshed family* situations that can arise. A mother or father may favor a particular child and use him or her as an ally, leading to serious consequences for the children and the parents.

6. Jacob's father, Isaac, experienced the trauma of being *bound* by *his* father, Abraham (Genesis 22). This experience represented Isaac's obedience and trust in the face of an unfathomable situation. Undoubtedly, this event had a great effect on Jacob's psyche. In many families, children need to deal with parents who have gone through great *trials and tribulations* in their own lives.

7. Jacob's beloved son, *Joseph*, was lost for a long period of time and mourned by his father. Many parents mourn the *unfulfilled potential* of one or more children, regarding such offspring as a lost future and an unredeemed promise. Furthermore, Joseph's experience in Egypt illustrates that there is always *a hidden meaning to one's destiny.* Joseph's enslavement and imprisonment turned out to be a blessing for him and his family. As Joseph stated: "...God meant it for good..." (Genesis 50:20).

8. The *barrenness* that afflicted Rachel (and Leah, temporarily) may be viewed as one of those unforeseen *illnesses* and difficulties that strike all individuals and families at one time or another.

These selected experiences drawn from Jacob's life cover the full spectrum of living -- the entire life cycle. Jacob encountered each of these specific challenges, yet similar events occur in the life of every individual. Every person struggles to harmonize internal and external aspects of the self. That is the nature of the human condition.

However, like Jacob, we can also understand that God is always present. That is what the Prophet Micah meant when he said that Jacob's "truth" would be passed on to succeeding generations. Each generation struggles, yet knows that it is not alone -- God is present.

Jacob's struggles continue to resonate within each and every one of us, helping to define our own humanness. Our Rabbis said (Talmud, *Taanit* 5b) that Jacob, our Father, has not died. Certainly, the voice and values of Jacob the Patriarch continue eternally. On a deeper level, our contemporary experiences can be seen to parallel those of Jacob. We can understand that our internal conflicts -- between public and private persona, conscious and unconscious self, realist and dreamer -- reflect aspects of Jacob. The struggle towards healing and towards wholeness is a central part of our human experience, just as it was for Jacob. Like Jacob, we understand that once healing is achieved internally, it becomes manifest externally also. Thus, we can achieve our own truth.

Jacob chose to be remembered not by the words of his response to the Pharaoh, reflecting his struggles, but rather in a positive and loving fashion. He was, after all, the "whole person, dwelling in tents." We should understand how Jacob chose to act at the end of his life, which determined the image by which he is remembered for all time. Frequently, the way that a life ends reflects how that life was lived. As Jacob was near death, he chose to bestow *blessings* on his children. That is how he wanted to be remembered throughout the generations.

The fact that Jacob gave each of his children discrete blessings, tailored to their unique, individual qualities, illustrates one of Jacob's strengths. He had psychological insight, which allowed him to appraise the distinct qualities of each of his children. He knew his children and his descendants well, just as he knew himself. He recognized the uniqueness of every child and every person. This recognition is reflected in the Biblical statement that Jacob "blessed them; every one according to his blessing" (Genesis 49:28).

Most of the traditional Rabbinical commentaries agree that the blessings given by Jacob refer to the end of days, the period ushering in the Messianic era. Our ultimate human hope is to harmonize our internal and external goals and so, find our own truth. We must also recognize that despite the challenges we encounter in life, God is with us. He gave that blessing and guarantee of His eternal Presence to Jacob, who transmitted it to his children and grandchildren, down to each of us in our time.

Jacob is considered the *Shalem she-be-Avot* (Genesis 33:18), the most complete Patriarch, because an understanding of his experience helps us harmonize our internal and external selves. It is fitting that the final Torah Portion concerning Jacob is called *Vayehi*, "And he [Jacob] lived." Jacob, our Patriarch, has not died. In his life experiences, and in his blessings, he continues to live on eternally and to bless and enrich our lives.

Jacob always felt that God was with him, so it was natural for him to spend the last moments of his life giving blessings to his children that would pass down to their descendants until the end of days. In addition to recognizing God's Presence, Jacob also heard the voice of his grandfather, Abraham, across the generations. God appeared to Abraham many years before, telling him to "be a blessing" (Genesis 12:2) and to "be whole" (Genesis 17:1). Those messages guided Jacob along his path. They can also be heard by each of us, in every generation, guiding us to a meaningful, harmonious life of truth and blessing.

CHAPTER II

GOD'S STRUGGLE WITH MAN: JACOB AND THE LONELY NIGHT JOURNEY

And Jacob was left alone, and an *Ish* struggled with him until dawn. And the *Ish* saw that he could not overcome Jacob, and he touched the cavity of Jacob's thigh, and he dislodged Jacob's hip joint as he was struggling with him. And the *Ish* said: 'Let me go, for dawn has already arrived,' and Jacob said to the *Ish*: 'Our struggle will continue into daylight until you bless me.' And the *Ish* said to Jacob: 'What is your name?,' and he said: 'My name is Jacob.' And the *Ish* said: 'Jacob shall not be your exclusive name; you will also be known as Israel, because you have prevailed with God and with men.' And Jacob asked the *Ish*: 'Please tell me your name,' and the *Ish* said: 'Why are you asking for my name?,' and the *Ish* blessed Jacob there. And Jacob designated the name of the place as Peniel, which acknowledged that 'I was privileged to see God face to face, and my life was spared.' And as Jacob passed Penuel, the sun shone for him, and Jacob limped on his thigh. Therefore, the Children of Israel shall forever not eat the sinew of the thigh-vein, which is on the hollow of the thigh, precisely because the *Ish* dislodged the hollow of Jacob's thigh, in the thigh-vein. (Genesis 32:25-33)

I

INTRODUCTION

I have always been perplexed by the fact that the Jewish people are known as *Bnei Yisrael* (the Children of Israel). It is self-evident that the term "Children of Israel" derives from the fact that the children of Jacob (Israel) became the Twelve Tribes of Israel. My query, however, is an attempt to understand this appellation on a more profound level. For example, one could hypothesize that the name for the Jewish people might be *Bnei Avraham* (the Children of Abraham) or *Bnei Moshe* (the Children of Moses).

After all, Abraham was the first person to rediscover monotheism and was also known as the Father of nations. One of his attributes was that he performed acts of lovingkindness. So the name "Children of Abraham" would have served as an inspiration to future generations. Furthermore, Abraham also went through a metamorphosis. First, he was known as Avram. Then his name was changed to reflect his mission to the world and his essence, i.e., the Father of all nations (Genesis 17:5).

Similarly, the name "Children of Moses" also seems appropriate. Moses was the greatest of all the Prophets, and he served as the mediator between God and the Jewish people at the time of Revelation and the giving of the Torah.

But the Jewish people are not known by the names of these ancestors, although interestingly, our Christian and Islamic brethren frequently refer to the Jewish people as the Children of Abraham. We refer to ourselves exclusively as the *Bnei Yisrael* (Children of Israel). Despite this appellation, when the blessings are given to the Twelve Tribes by their father (Genesis 49), he is referred to as Jacob, not Israel. Perhaps this choice of names is to illustrate that in achieving the fulfillment of these blessings, each of us needs to work through our own process of becoming who we are destined to be.

One of the first times that we are referred to as the Children of Israel is in Genesis 46:8, when the Bible enumerates those who go down to Egypt. Apparently, this reference suggests the importance of the descent into Egypt, as well as the essence of what Israel actually stands for. That essence will serve as the vehicle for the future redemption from exile.

The descent into Egypt may be understood on many levels. First, although the Children of Israel were uprooted from their own land, Egypt initially provided them with material sustenance. Second, the etymology of the Hebrew word for Egypt (*Mitzrayim*) is related to the word *tzar* ("narrow," "dangerous"), perhaps signifying that the people were entering narrow and dangerous straits, a place of oppression and difficulties. Third, the name of Egypt is associated with what happened there, i.e., an enslavement that was both physical and psychological.

In order to understand what the name "Children of Israel" signifies regarding the individual and collective destiny of the people, we need to understand the change of name from "Jacob our Patriarch" to Israel. We must also keep in mind that one name was not totally eclipsed in favor of the other. Israel was bestowed as an additional name for Jacob. Thus, when we refer to Jacob, we are aware that we also refer to Israel, and vice versa.

How did Jacob come to also be Israel? While Jacob was preparing to meet his brother, he experienced a *numinous* event that ultimately would change the entire direction of his own path, as well as that of the entire Jewish people.

Prior to Jacob's encounter during the night, he found himself entirely alone. The thoughts that passed through his mind at that silent and lonely time might have included a review of his entire life until then. This was a mid-life evaluation of who he was, a survey of his goals and reflections about his lineage, i.e., his parents and grandparents.

His questions to himself might have included the following: "What was my destiny supposed to be as the twin born second, holding on to the heel of Esau? Was sibling rivalry a motivating factor in my obtaining the birthright? Was I preying on the vulnerability of my brother, who was tired and hungry? Why did I listen to my mother and receive the blessing of my father, when Esau was out doing my father's bidding? More perplexing, who was my father and who was my mother? Was my father, Isaac, really spared, or was a part of him symbolically sacrificed on the altar? Was he a victor or a victim? Why didn't my father and mother communicate about such crucial matters?" Interestingly, only one conversation between Isaac and Rebekah is recorded in the Bible, in Genesis 27:46.

"I understand that my mother received a prophecy regarding the blessing that was to be bestowed upon me. Is prophecy supposed to be kept a secret between husband and wife? Does the course of destiny trample on marital etiquette in a relationship? Can a blessing emerge out of secrecy?

Perhaps when I meet my brother, Esau, he actually will kill me, and I will die prematurely. Has my life been fulfilled? Have I been honest with myself, with my family, with God? I recognize that God has given me unparalleled visionary opportunities -- a Ladder of Ascension; Isaac for a father; Abraham for a grandfather; a lineage that is blessed."

Jacob's encounter with Esau after he crosses the Yabok River finds its symbolism represented in each of our lives as well. We are engaged in a continual process of self-evaluation. We ask ourselves similar questions before the major encounters in our lives. These encounters do not have to involve confrontations with brothers or other family members bent on murder. They can involve, for example, issues such as illness, bankruptcy, aloneness, loneliness, depression, anxiety or mere fright.

At its core, the encounter between Jacob and Esau focuses on the fear of the other. Jacob perceives Esau as someone who is bigger, more powerful and more authoritative than he. Moreover, he recognizes that Esau is someone with whom he consciously or unconsciously acted in bad faith, and someone whom he hugged and kissed, but perhaps not wholeheartedly.

"People know me as a person who dwells in tents, studying and meditating. But there is another side of me as well. I am jealous of my brother; I do not know how to hunt, as he does. Furthermore, why did my father love my brother, while my mother loved me? There is a dark side of me that is not revealed to others, but is known to me. I wanted to marry Rachel; she is my beloved. But first I had to marry Leah. My uncle tricked me. Just look at my uncle's name, Laban. It means "white," signifying purity. To outsiders, he is known as 'pure,' but he cheated me. Perhaps I focused on my uncle's externals, with too much trust.

"Then what did God do? My favorite wife was barren, and I kept having children that I initially did not want. I am confused. I love and I do not love. My destiny often seems to be at odds with my desires. What good was my dream about the Ladder of Ascension if it was followed by Laban ('White') being deceitful to me?

"Here I am, stuck at the Yabok river, with many confusing and bothersome thoughts. Maybe I should end my life. Or, perhaps the water is here to remind me of its symbolism for life, creation and the unconscious. Furthermore, I know that I am not supposed to die here. By its name, the Yabok (from the root, *avak*, 'to struggle') tells me that I am here merely to struggle.

"Perhaps what will happen between me and my brother will foretell the history of the world. Why must the blessing that my father gave be through 'me' alone and not through 'us?' Maybe I can create an 'us.' My struggles and thoughts will play a role in the destiny of the Jewish people and the world. But perhaps I am not in charge, as I have seen, for instance, regarding my marriage. Perhaps Divine Providence will guide me on my way. Before the Dream of Ascension, I prayed to God, and now, before my encounter in the night, I am all alone again, to pray to God."

Reflections on the Struggle

One of the reasons that this section of the Torah is significant for me, particularly in my adulthood, is related to the date on which this portion is read annually in the synagogue. Eighteen days after my father went into a coma, following a heart attack, he died on the 17th of the Hebrew month of Kislev. The anniversary of his death (*Yahrzeit*) usually falls on or near the Sabbath on which the portion that includes these verses is read. For each of these eighteen years since his death, I have been asked to give a Torah-related talk or lesson related to this section. It is as if God has asked me to look at these passages with particular care.

Does individual growth take place with family members present, or with rabbis or doctors present, or does it take place when one is alone? Before the world was created, how did God feel? Was He lonely or alone? Was His feeling of loneliness alleviated through creating other entities, or was the loneliness accentuated by the qualitative differences between God and His creations? Does God continue to be alone? Is God in search of man, or vice versa? Or both?

Jacob was alone, both physically and spiritually. Sometimes, one can be alone and not lonely. One can also be lonely, even though not alone. Jacob felt both lonely and alone.

Are loneliness and aloneness a deviation, or are they the norm of an ordinary life? Although we, as a society, place emphasis and value on friendship, family, local community and world community, ultimately we live in solitude, constantly reflecting, contemplating, even while enjoying life.

To some, the word "solitude" has negative connotations, but this term is not used here in a negative sense. Rather, it is meant to convey an empirical, psychological observation about life. It is meant to illustrate the specialness, uniqueness and distinctiveness of each individual's psyche and private thoughts.

Even in intimacy, when two become one, they still remain two. The Torah focuses on two becoming one in a physical sense ("and they shall be one flesh," Genesis 2:24); however, this does not include the merger of individual psyches. Even when two become one physically, in their psychological existence, each maintains his or her own thoughts and identities. They share these parts of themselves, to the extent that they want to, and when they deem this to be appropriate.

Each individual is also alone with his or her own image of God. This image constantly changes throughout one's life. Each person's relationship with God is unique. It is natural to be angry with God at times, just as it is natural to experience all types of feelings, from happiness to fear, in this relationship.

One is also alone with one's dreams and fantasies. In the moments before Jacob's encounter, he is alone, and a unique struggle then begins. That struggle has meaning and significance for the future -- for the Jewish people and humanity in general.

Jacob's struggle takes place during the night. The terms of the struggle are carefully delineated; it must end before the light of the next day, at dawn. The nighttime of the struggle is not meant to refer to the hours of darkness of that night. Rather, it could represent a period of darkness in the life of a person. That time period could be weeks, months or even years. No matter how much light that person is exposed to, this interval is his or her own nighttime.

A similar thought is expressed in the Passover *Haggadah*, in the famous question: "How is this night different from all other nights?" There are multifaceted interpretations of this central question of the Seder night. One interpretation suggests: "How is this exile different from other exiles that the Jewish people have experienced?"

The lonely night journey represents one's exile from one's self. When one is in this type of exile, it always feels like nighttime. One is engaged in a deep struggle, never knowing or anticipating the dawn of light and hope.

How does one feel in the midst of the darkness of exile? One is aware that the rest of the world is asleep, unaware of other people's plights, unaware of the agony and the sense of alienation being experienced by others. No *festive* meals or family gatherings ever take place during this lonely and dark time. One's only source of light during these moments is provided by looking heavenward, to the stars and the galaxies. However, contemplating the distance to those heavenly bodies only accentuates the sufferer's feelings of inadequacy, which can almost annihilate the individual. This period of nighttime seems never-ending, with no past and no future, only an eternal present of hopelessness and despair.

Equally deafening is the stillness of the night, in which almost all stimuli are diminished. At night, even if one is surrounded by noise, friends or conversation, one nevertheless sometimes feels so isolated as to be immune to external stimuli, since they seem to have no connection to the internal life. Ultimately, this lonely night journey represents the epitome of fear of the unknown -- of what is, what is to come, and what must be faced and learned about oneself.

"And a man (*Ish*) struggled with him." This "man" has no specific identity. This *Ish* without an identity is found only in a few other places in the entire Bible. One occurrence is in Genesis 18:2, where three "men" come to visit Abraham. Another is Genesis 37:15, where an *Ish* directs Joseph to where he can find his brothers. Another instance is in Exodus 2:12, where Moses, before he smites the Egyptian, looks around and sees that there is no *Ish*. Later on, in Judges 13:11, an *Ish* appears to Manoah and his wife, bearing news of the forthcoming birth of Samson.

In the case of Jacob's encounter, since the *Ish* has no specific identity, Biblical commentators throughout the ages have given the *Ish* various identities. Some say that he represents that which is externally hostile to Jacob, i.e., the image of Esau. Some commentators say that this *Ish* represents what is internally adverse to Jacob -- the dark, shadowy, trickster side of Jacob. And some commentators say that this *Ish* represents the dark Image of God (Genesis *Rabbah* 77:3; Rashi and Rashbam on Genesis 32:25).

All three of these interpretations actually say the same thing, namely that Jacob was struggling with diverse aspects of himself. However, the Torah emphasizes that this encounter was with an *Ish*. This struggle could have been with another person, or with Jacob himself or with an angel of God taking the form of a human being. In one other place in the Bible, Judges 13:16, this *Ish* is identified as an angel of God. Another understanding of "angel of God" is "messenger of God." The messenger of God usually takes the form of a person.

I think that the Torah wants to emphasize a lesson for all generations to come. We also encounter angels of God throughout our lifetime. However, we do not always know who these persons may be. Perhaps they are those we would least expect to really help us or guide us. Therefore, we have to be specifically attuned to the unanticipated. We have to always be aware, knowing that a person we encounter may be representative of a Divine message. This approach and attitude will naturally heighten our consciousness of every experience we have, every person crossing our path, every message and song we hear and every article we read.

II

BECOMING ONE AND WHOLE

What was Jacob's struggle? He was aware that perhaps he was facing his own mortality. He was aware that ultimately, justice might prevail. He was aware that lentil soup does not buy one the status of firstborn. He was aware that there was deception, even if preordained by Divine prophecy to Rebekah, in his receiving a blessing from his father.

He was aware that one cannot go on living a life of deception. He was aware that he wanted to make peace with his Creator.

The external threat of Jacob's meeting with his archenemy -- his brother, his twin -- revitalized the realization that before his possible death, he would want to be whole and at peace with himself. The possibility of his death was the catalyst for Jacob's internal struggle, the struggle of becoming one and whole, and of recognizing that one of the Patriarchs cannot build the Jewish people on a foundation of deceit that is ignored. Jacob was becoming increasingly conscious of the fact that what is ultimately required of each person is a metamorphosis and transformation as an individual human being.

No individual can ultimately rely on his or her lineage, even if that lineage includes Abraham and Isaac. No individual can ultimately rely on a mother, even if she is a Rebekah, who receives private prophecy. No family situation and no circumstances of birth, childhood or young adulthood can be the determining factor of who one becomes. One cannot say: "I am the firstborn," or "I am the middle child," or "I am the last-born," and therefore attribute one's fate in life to birth order. Similarly, one cannot attribute one's destiny to having been favored by a mother or a father. Neither, for that matter, can one say that the future is determined by the constellation of stars at the time of birth, or by a famine endured in one's youth or by a Holocaust that one has survived.

Each person is ultimately responsible for what he or she becomes. Each person has to identify with his or her own struggle with Esau, i.e., one's dark side, or with shameful or embarrassing aspects of one's past. This struggle may take the form of a repetitive dream that has never been acted upon. A recurring dream may convey an important conceptual message, to which the dreamer has not listened or responded. Hopefully, during one's lifetime, while one is healthy, he or she will engage in a Jacob-like struggle of self-determination.

Jacob's struggle with Esau finds its analogue in contemporary life. Interestingly, Jacob's struggle was not initially metaphysical. At the outset, it was between him and his brother, his twin, so that it was a family struggle. Furthermore, it was a struggle that emanated from maternal nepotism in favor of Jacob and paternal nepotism in favor of Esau. This was almost a classic case of family enmeshment. Often I hear, both in my office and at patients' bedsides, the tremendous alienation, isolation and loneliness that people experience within the family context. Sometimes brothers and sisters have not spoken for years. Or, if they have spoken, there has been only speech from the mind, uttered politely, rather than words from the heart, spoken authentically.

Often I hear about a domineering mother and a weak father image or vice versa. This is one way that an adult-child constantly transfers the blame and fault for his or her own inadequacies in life. Frequently I hear how the umbilical cord has never been severed psychologically. Frequently the dissolution of a marriage is blamed on early childhood experiences, e.g., having a narcissistic mother or father. Frequently I am told that a person's struggles are due to abandonment by a mother or a father. Frequently I hear how "my father was an alcoholic and he abused me." Frequently I hear of all types of experiences that people use as justification for unhappiness, anxiety, fearfulness and impotence. Interestingly, these complaints that I hear from people in their thirties or forties are identical with the observations of people in their seventies, particularly among those who face imminent death. Jacob's struggle is a perennial and paradigmatic struggle for each individual.

Darkness and Dawn

Jacob's struggle takes place during complete darkness. At the first arrival of light, the struggle automatically terminates. Is it not odd that while Jacob is in the midst of the struggle, he already knows when it will end? Jacob's struggle during the darkness epitomizes the dichotomy between one's public persona (meaning "mask") and one's private, individual struggles.

During daytime hours, people are well dressed and publicly polite; at times they may smile or laugh. They usually adapt to the appropriate social etiquette. During daytime hours, the emphasis is on social conformity and on not creating too many upheavals within the family or community unit. A person's professional title is the identification by which he or she is known. Habitual routines provide a sense of security and a predictable pattern of living. Nonconformity is usually perceived as an expression of boldness, assertiveness or aggressiveness.

But these daytime identities are masks that everyone wears. Every mask is dependent on the culture and society in which one is raised. However, all masks are removed in the darkness and stillness of the night. When one's public identity is removed, very fundamental and essential questions and struggles emerge, such as: "Who am I? Where am I going? How can I integrate my past with my present and my future? What is my destiny? Where is my personal God? What is my true experience of life and God, and who are my significant friends and family? What are my fears?"

Jacob, like everyone else, feels the enormous gap between his public life -- which seemingly even has the approval of Divine Providence -- and his innermost, internal struggle with life per se. The arrival of dawn not only coincides with the end of the struggle, but also perhaps represents a gradual integration of the public and the private individual. Perhaps the light is the first ray of the hope of redemption, where darkness and light can merge together. The darkness can shed meaning on the light and vice versa. Together, they constellate to create a new phenomenon called *the oneness and unity of life*.

Why did Jacob's struggle take place specifically in the darkness? What was his association with darkness? Jacob was constantly aware of how he had received the blessing of his father, thereby continuing in the tradition of Abraham and Isaac. Jacob was able to receive the blessing only because of Isaac's blindness, i.e., a form of nighttime. Isaac could feel and hear his son but could not see him.

For Jacob, the darkness on the night of the encounter with the *Ish* conjured up memories of how he had received his father's blessing by using deception. Jacob, the "whole person, dwelling in tents," had added darkness to his father's blindness. When one carries around memories such as this, the nighttime is inevitably unsettling.

What went through Jacob's mind regarding his father? Jacob may have said to himself: "How often I have heard that my father was a survivor of an attempted sacrifice. How often I have been told that his life was spared just as *his* father was about to sacrifice him on the altar. My father's life was saved literally by one second. Will I have the same fate? What will the *Ish* do to me? Will he turn into an angel and intercede for me as an angel did for my father, or will I be sacrificed on the altar of Yabok?

"Why did my father always have to remind me that he almost was sacrificed? I have grown up as a product of the second generation, fearful of being born and of surviving. I really am a 'whole person, dwelling in tents.' Did I start this struggle? No. The *Ish* initiated it. If the *Ish* represents a form of God in whatever guise, why is God struggling with man?

"The darkness is not complete, however. I am able to see a glimpse of the moon. There is some light. The *lunar* sphere is visible. I am reminded that perhaps I am a complete *lunatic*. So little light plunges me into more darkness. Perhaps I am imagining this whole thing, yet it hurts."

Things always look easier before they are attempted. In this case, the *Ish* initiated a fight and the *Ish* was the adversary. One would think that the *Ish* would only undertake such a mission if he felt he could prevail easily and quickly. There is always such a difference between observing life and living life. When one observes life and evaluates the pros and cons of a situation, one sometimes finds logical and rational solutions with great clarity. But in living life, the burdens of suffering, pain, grief, mourning and loss always overcome one with their intensity. The compassion and empathy of friends and family, as welcome as these qualities are, can never really overcome a person's private emotional experience.

I do not know whether this *Ish*'s initial plan was to kill Jacob -- to sacrifice him on the altar of Yabok -- or just to defeat him in a struggle. I do not know what is meant by "to be defeated in a struggle." Is it conceivable that the *Ish*, a Divine messenger in human form, was attempting once again to have a human sacrifice, and this time he was actually accomplishing it himself? Was this God's struggle with Jacob, or with the Divine Self? Does God need or want sacrifices, be they animal or human?

The *Ish* that Jacob encounters is known in Midrashic literature as either the "Prince of Jacob" or God Himself. Thus, he represents the most lofty and highest aspect of an individual who confronts the dark and shadow side of an individual. Why did this *Ish* begin a struggle with Jacob? Did he exhaust all of the other alternatives? Did he attempt a dialogue with Jacob? Did he attempt softness, tenderness and love? Or, did this lofty and elevated *Ish* show his dark side by initially struggling and fighting with Jacob?

III

ESAU AND JACOB

Unable to physically prevail over Jacob, the *Ish* causes him an indelible disability, a permanent sign that will remain with Jacob for the rest of his life, causing him to limp. The hip joint connects the upper and lower parts of a person's body. An injury to that joint affects one's weight-bearing capabilities, so that Jacob's body weight is suddenly felt to be a burden every time he takes a step. There is a new image of Jacob limping. This is the outer expression of his weakness and vulnerability. His inner transformation, signified by his limping, is what makes possible Esau's reaction to him. Instead of attacking and killing Jacob, Esau is able to kiss him and to cry.

The Torah's statement, "and Esau kissed Jacob" (Genesis 33:4), is one of the ten places in the Torah where there are special markings within or above a word. Where the text reads "and he kissed him," there is a dot above each of the Hebrew letters. There is a beautiful Midrash regarding this matter:

> So said Ezra: "If Elijah comes and says to me, 'Why did you write in this manner?,' I will say to him: 'I have already placed dots on top [and therefore I cannot erase the words].' And if he says to me, 'How nicely this is written,' I will remove the dots from on top of the words. (*Abot de Rabbi Natan*, Schechter ed., 51, 1 6-49, 2).

What this Midrash expresses is that no matter how many generations pass, or how difficult it may be for people to understand this passage, the text regarding Esau's kissing Jacob will never be altered. In the encounter with Jacob, Esau takes the initiative in embracing Jacob. Esau is able to perceive the changed Jacob. Perhaps he even knows that Jacob's name is also Israel.

Another Midrash presents an alternate interpretation of the dots, suggesting that although Esau dislikes Jacob, he kisses him sincerely. The Midrash states:

> Rabbi Simeon bar Yohai says: "It is a well established principle that Esau [and that which is symbolized by him] dislikes Jacob. However, his emotions overwhelmed him and he kissed his brother with a full heart and sincerity." (*Sifre*, Numbers 69, Horovitz edition, p. 64)

The first Midrash anticipates the second one. Ezra has an intuition that despite the fact that the Torah says "and Esau kissed Jacob," later commentators may cast doubt on the authenticity and sincerity of this embrace and kiss.

The second Midrash is a fulfillment of the essential doubt concerning what is meant by the embrace and kiss. First, Esau's kissing is seen as ambivalent. Second, even if Esau's kissing is seen as sincere, one is cautioned from regarding Esau's and Jacob's behavior as a symbolic paradigm for the future of Gentile and Jewish relationships.

I, however, would like to believe that Ezra's interpretation contains the seeds of the Messianic ideal of the brotherhood of humanity. The message for eternity is that opposites and adversaries should be able to find unity despite their diverse outlooks. Hopefully, opposites can not only be tolerated, but also respected. Even when an irreconcilable clash emerges, the parties can respectfully agree to disagree.

As noted above, in Jacob's encounter with the *Ish*, he becomes changed both physically and psychologically. Jacob's limp is noticeable not just to him; it will always be visible to everyone else. Jacob will represent a living symbol of a most unusual struggle. During this struggle, does the *Ish* become hurt, or is he always on the offensive?

Furthermore, who is this *Ish*? If the *Ish* fighting with Jacob is a human being, this struggle can take place at night and continue into the daytime, as well. However, the description of the adversary as an *Ish* can be interpreted as a literary device to hint at the *Ish*'s true identity as an Image of God. This strange power that initiates a struggle with Jacob functions specifically during the nighttime, so that the vast multitudes of people will not recognize this unusual aspect of the dark Image of God.

This *Ish*, although he dislodges Jacob's hip, continues to struggle. When the struggle seems endless and the dawn approaches, the assailant quickly decides to present a polite aspect of himself, saying: "We will resume our struggle later, but right now we both need to resume our normal activities, because daytime is approaching."

Jacob is well aware of the treacherous power of the *Ish*. He remembers how, years before, he was foiled when, with all his heart and soul, he wanted to marry Rachel. During that other nighttime experience, Jacob was tricked into marrying Leah, rather than his beloved Rachel. Was it only his Uncle Laban who deceived Jacob? Or, was it through the atmosphere of darkness surrounding that evening that Jacob was somehow deceived? Jacob has learned to fear the nighttime, as a time when he can be deceived and when he sometimes loses control over what happens to him.

Blessing

During Jacob's encounter, he is aware that the *Ish* is capable of more than causing tremendous physical and psychological difficulties. Somehow, precisely because of these difficulties, Jacob can transform them into a blessing. It is at this juncture of the struggle, precisely at the first ray of dawn's light, that Jacob begins to have the upper hand in the struggle. Interestingly, Jacob does not want to take vengeance on the *Ish*. Rather, he desires a blessing from him.

What is a blessing? A blessing that one receives from God remains eternal. A blessing gives one guidance and support in multidimensional ways. A blessing (*berakhah*) adds humility to a person's character, since the root of the word relates to the knee and bending. The greatest blessing comes about when specifically, your adversary can bless you.

Apparently, the process of blessing begins when the adversary asks his opponent what his name is. At this point, Jacob feels completely startled. He knows that his grandfather's name was changed from Avram to Avraham (Genesis 17:5). He knows that his grandmother's name was changed from Sarai to Sarah (Genesis 17:15). And he realizes that the name changes of his grandparents were very significant. His grandfather became the Father of the multitude of nations. Not only the Israelites, but the Arabs, are descendants of Abraham. Furthermore, the name of his grandmother, Sarah, also indicates that she is a Matriarch for all. Both of his grandparents had their names changed to indicate a shift from the particular to the universal. Both in Biblical literature and in Aristotelian philosophy, the names of animals, plants and persons signify and designate the essence of the matter.

Jacob thinks: "Is my name going to be changed? I was not the firstborn. I am called 'Yaakov' (Jacob) because I held on to Esau's heel. Then I deceptively gained the rights of the firstborn. My name 'Yaakov' means 'trickster, supplanter,' indicating that I received the blessing from my father that was supposed to go to my brother, Esau. I have my own feelings about the significance of being firstborn. Can't every child be considered and treated like a firstborn? Can't every child receive a coat of many colors? Can't the diamond of every child be discovered and polished? Can't ancestral blessings be bestowed on both children, Jacob and Esau, Isaac and Ishmael? Why does there have to be nepotism, creating a situation where certain children are excluded?"

By responding to the *Ish*, "my name is Jacob," Jacob admits that his past includes very dark and deceptive parts of his life. At the same moment, he is aware that perhaps his Uncle Laban's tricking him into marrying Leah was punishment for Jacob's own deception. Jacob realizes that the foundation of the Jewish people will never endure without coming to terms with who Jacob is and what he did to secure the ancestral blessings. Jacob is aware that what he perpetrated in deceiving Esau and Isaac was the heinous crime of psychological betrayal.

The blessing that Jacob receives takes the form of Jacob's being given an additional name, a new identity. No longer will Jacob constantly feel guilty, trying to wash the blood of deception from his hands. He will be able to stand erect, proud of who he is and who he was, a man guided by a mysterious Divine force and one who has become a progenitor of the Jewish people.

However, Jacob is somewhat unsure of what the name "Israel" means. He initially thinks that he is connected to his grandmother, Sarai, as he becomes the "Sar El," the Prince of God. But his doubts are resolved when the *Ish* elaborates on the exact meaning of his new name and identity of Israel.

The *Ish*'s explanation to Jacob, "that you have prevailed with God and with men," gives Jacob courage in approaching his brother, Esau. Jacob has a visceral feeling that this lonely night journey will serve him well. However, the name "Israel" has an even more profound meaning for Jacob. Not only does he feel comforted concerning his future encounter with Esau, but also he feels that his honest encounter with the *Ish* allowed him to do battle with God, leaving him limping, yet victorious.

Jacob now has a new realization of the multiple Images of God. One past Image was quite beautiful for him, when he had his dream (Genesis 28) about the Ladder of Ascension. There, the angels of God were seen ascending and descending, and they promised Jacob that God would always be with him and his descendants. But, in this case, Jacob has another Image of God. This time, He is seen in the form of an *Ish*, who initiates struggles with individuals. Jacob is therefore able to have a composite picture of the Divine. Consequently, he does not have to ask the perennial questions, "Why me? Why now?" Jacob realizes that God is present in the beauty of life, but also in the struggles of life.

Jacob is also aware that his name is not only Israel, but also Jacob. This realization is that which is echoed by King David: "My sin, my history, who I am can always be transcended, but can never be eliminated" (Psalms 51:5). Jacob realizes that, "I am Israel, and I have prevailed with God and with men [both Esau and Laban], but I am also Jacob. These multiple identities will be with me throughout my life."

Jacob's question regarding the *Ish*'s name is quite different from the question the *Ish* put to him. Jacob structures his sentence politely and uses the word *na*, "please," though the *Ish* uses no niceties. Why does Jacob want to know the *Ish*'s name? Is this a matter of cordial reciprocity? Or, does Jacob audaciously plan to bless the *Ish* by giving him an additional name?

Jacob is certainly to be commended for having the forbearance and presence of mind in this encounter to ask for the *Ish*'s name. At this point, is Jacob foreshadowing Moses's request to know the Name of God (Exodus 3:14)? When Moses asks for God's Name, God tells him that "I am that I am." That is, the Image of God will continuously change for each individual throughout his or her lifetime.

When Jacob asks for the name of the *Ish*, he is rebuked by that Divine messenger, who responds: "Why are you asking for my Name?" As previously indicated, this *Ish* appears numerous times in the Bible, but nowhere is his true identity revealed. However, upon closer scrutiny, it may be that his lack of identity represents the same truth that was revealed to Moses, i.e., "I am that I am." In one instance, the *Ish* appears to Jacob as an adversary. However, this same *Ish* appears to Joseph and directs him to his brothers. And the *Anashim* (a plural form of *Ish*) who come to visit Abraham have multiple identities. So perhaps the *Ish*'s identity is, in fact, "I am that I am."

I am puzzled by the *Ish*'s blessing Jacob at the conclusion of their encounter (Genesis 32:30). I thought that the blessing had already taken place through Jacob's name being changed to Israel. Yet, I doubt that this latter blessing is a recapitulation of the first one. I hypothesize that after changing Jacob's name and speaking with Jacob about his own concealed name, the *Ish* gave Jacob an additional blessing, whose contents are not revealed to us. However, I would like to speculate about the content of this blessing. Jacob wanted to know the identity of this *Ish*. Jacob wanted and needed support, not a physical cane to support his limping leg, but rather a spiritual cane that would allow Jacob to derive everlasting meaning from God's struggle with him. In this second blessing, he received an eternal spiritual blessing.

IV

EXPERIENCING THE DIVINE

Jacob designated the name of the place of the encounter as "Peniel," acknowledging that he had been privileged to see God face to face. He further acknowledged that in this process, his life had been spared.

In order to understand this central sentence relating to Jacob's perception of the whole struggle, it is necessary to examine Exodus 33, sentences 17 through 23. After the episode of the Golden Calf and the breaking of the first Tablets of the Law, Moses asks to have the unique privilege of understanding the honor of God. God reveals to Moses His moral attributes of mercy and compassion. But He says that the ultimate understanding of God shall remain unfathomable to Moses and to every other mortal. He tells Moses that "you will be able to understand My back, but the essence of who I am, represented by My *face*, shall remain impenetrable." Thus, what God says to Moses is that despite all human strivings -- of intellect, emotion and spirit -- there shall always remain a partial eclipse of God.

Moses, as the greatest of the Prophets, *knew* God *"face to face"* (Exodus 33:11, Deuteronomy 34:10 and Numbers 12:8). These citations, however, merely describe the status of Moses's prophecy, indicating how it differed from that of the other Prophets. Moses's prophecy was more intimate and more direct, although even he was not allowed to see the face of God.

Indeed, one of the thirteen Principles of Faith, recited daily, is the declaration of the uniqueness of Moses's prophecy. Biblical commentators are, therefore, very troubled in explaining Jacob's actually seeing God face to face. The *Targum Onkelos* tries to reconcile this contradiction by saying that Jacob saw the face of the angel, but not of God.

When it comes to a request for the cognitive understanding of God, such as that put forth by Moses, one cannot obtain a satisfactory response, i.e., cognition of a Divine Being. However, Jacob's request was not cognitive. He was describing his *experience* of struggling with the darkness of God Himself.

The distinction between cognition and experience is essential. While cognition refers to an epistemological comprehension of God, which is *ipso facto* limited, an experience, of necessity, allows one to come to various Images of God. That is why everyone's life journey is unique, singular and incomparable to anyone else's life journey.

The experience of life is unique to each individual. Each person has his or her own mode of thinking and reflecting, conscious and unconscious thoughts, complexities of the psyche, fantasies and dreams. Only through subjectivity in defining the essence of the human being, can one say: "I have been privileged to see the face of God in totality." The seemingly unbridgeable gap between humanity and divinity can be overcome only through a deepening of one's self, as one struggles with the multiple Images of God in one's life.

Varying Images of God are recounted throughout the Biblical narrative. Moses uses a very strong and unique Image of the Divine in his Song of Gratitude after crossing the Sea of Reeds. In one verse (Exodus 15:3), composed after Moses and the Israelites witness the miraculous hand of God in the initial redemptive process, Moses declares that God is an *Ish* of War. This is the sole Biblical reference to God as an *Ish*. Perhaps this is similar to the Image of God that initiated the struggle with Jacob. The statement that God is not an *Ish* (Numbers 23:19) does not negate the aforementioned.

The Jacob in Us

The Bible does not tell us that the sun rose, but that it rose "for him," i.e., for Jacob. It rose for someone who had become Israel, who had received an unknown blessing and who had been privileged to see God face to face.

There is tremendous risk in exploring the unknown. The Talmud recounts the mystical explorations of four great Sages who wanted to discover the secrets of life (*Hagigah* 14b). Of these four, only Rabbi Akiba emerged peacefully. Ben Azzai looked too deeply and died; Ben Zoma looked too deeply and became demented; and Aher became an apostate.

However, other explorations are often regarded as essential to undertake. People often perceive danger in struggling with life and with God, yet each individual needs to examine these aspects of life.

Maimonides (*Mishneh Torah, Hilkhot Yesodei ha-Torah* 4:13) has an interesting suggestion in terms of one's development and growth. He states that before one undertakes an exploration of the mysteries of life, one should achieve external stability. The Talmud (*Sukkah* 28a) defines this achievement as having studied all of the questions of Abbaye and Rava regarding how one should conduct oneself in daily behavior and routine.

Both Maimonides and the Talmud suggest that the exploration of life should begin when one is approximately at mid-life, or what C. G. Jung refers to as the beginning of the second half of life. Jacob's encounter with the *Ish* constituted his mid-life journey. What happened to Jacob, when the sun shone for him, was the conceptual antecedent of Rabbi Akiba's experience. Jacob explored life in depth and became lame, yet the sun shone for him.

Avram's name was changed permanently to Avraham. Likewise, Sarai's name was changed permanently to Sarah. Only Jacob was given an *alternate* name, Israel. In the Book of Genesis, the names Jacob and Israel are frequently used interchangeably. These references indicate that there is a balance in life between opposing forces, such as light and darkness, or good and evil. Even though the sun shone for Jacob, the sun always sets; the sun does not shine permanently for anyone.

The text indicates that the sun shone for Jacob as he passed Peniel. The emphasis here is on the past tense. From this choice of verb, we learn that there is a difference between the moment something is experienced and the moments that follow. At the height of an experience, there may be confusion, or even chaos. Additional time is needed to integrate the new experience with one's prior knowledge.

Piaget refers to new, cognitive knowledge that needs to be integrated as the process of accommodation. What Jacob needed to do was to recognize that God can struggle with human beings. Both divinity and humanity can become victors; they both can become Israel.

In Jacob's encounter, the *Ish* was not defeated. A new Image of God appeared to Jacob. Therefore, we can say that the Image of God became enhanced for Jacob.

As mentioned above, Jacob's injury is visible to all. We, as the descendants of Jacob and the Children of Israel, have inherited his limp. For us, this limp represents the complexity of what it means to be human and Jewish and what it means to have an ever-changing relationship with God.

The Hebrew word used in the text for "limped" is *tzolea*. Through word association, one is reminded of the birth of Eve, the first woman. This birthing process (Genesis 2:21-22) is carried out using the *tzela* ("side" or "rib") of Adam. God's removal of Adam's rib is symbolic of a rebirth. Henceforth, there will be both man and woman.

In the creation story, Adam receives as a companion a woman (*Isha*) who is fashioned from his *tzela*. Similarly, the limping Jacob will forever be accompanied by Israel. Now, while Jacob limps, it will always be possible for each individual to struggle with God and see Him face to face.

The Thigh-Vein

Because the *Ish* dislodged the hollow of Jacob's thigh, the Children of Israel are prohibited forever from eating the sinew of the thigh-vein. This is the first Biblical reference to the Jewish people as the "Children of Israel." From this source, we learn that the first thing to remember, and remember eternally, is that we are the descendants of Jacob, but we need to become the Children of Israel.

Only three commandments to the Jewish people appear in the Book of Genesis, the Book that represents the foundation of the Torah, the Jewish people and humanity. The first commandment is to be fruitful and multiply in order to sustain the world. The second requires that all Jewish males undergo ritual circumcision, which constitutes a special covenant between God and the Jewish people. The third, and the first prohibition in the Torah, is the commandment that proscribes eating the sinew of the thigh-vein.

This commandment must be equal in importance to the other two commandments in Genesis. I suggest that this first prohibition serves as a constant reminder that Jacob's limp, and his transformation from Jacob into Israel, serves as a paradigm for each Jew. Through it, we are reminded that each of us has to go through a lonely night journey in becoming who we are destined to be.

V

THE LONELY NIGHT JOURNEY

Jacob's remaining alone and then going through the experience of his encounter is variously described as "the dark night of the soul," "the night sea journey," or "the hero's quest," a voyage which all must travel if they are driven toward the goal of realizing their creative potential.

Moses went through a similar journey. In the Book of Exodus, after accepting the mission to be the leader of the Jewish people, and after experiencing the numinosity of the Burning Bush, Moses has an encounter "*on the way*, at the lodging place" (Exodus 4:24). God appears to Moses, seeking to kill him because he has not circumcised his son. Moses's wife, Zipporah, saves his life, yet Moses experiences a "dark night of the soul." Here is a man who on one day is appointed leader of the Jewish people by God Himself, yet on the next day, experiences the possibility of his imminent death at the hand of God.

Jacob's experience and Moses's experience accentuate the fact that opposing forces of creative energy need to be recognized. Jacob feared the "Esau" energy, and Moses, a male, needed to recognize the feminine energy expressed by his wife, Zipporah.

Every person, in traveling along the journey of life, exposed to the hardships of life and the world, must depart from his or her family and from assorted collective traditions, as well as from self-imposed limitations. This journey requires courage. It ultimately allows everyone to live life to the fullest.

At the end of Jacob's life, as he bestows his paternal blessing on all of his children who will become the Twelve Tribes of Israel, he gathers them around his deathbed (Genesis 49:1-33). He seeks reassurance that the values of his grandfather and father, as well as his own values, will be carried on for generations to come.

Jacob wants the comfort of knowing that the Twelve Tribes of Israel will always be imbued with the covenantal promise. In unison, the sons, forming a circle around their father's bed, proclaim: "Hear, O Israel, the

Eternal our God: the Eternal is the Unique One." And when they say, "Hear, O Israel," their reference is not to the collective people of Israel, but to Jacob, their father.

Just before Jacob hears these reassuring words, he eloquently states that two of his grandchildren, Ephraim and Manasseh, the two sons of Joseph, are as dear to him as his own sons, Reuben and Simeon (Genesis 48:5). Indeed, Ephraim and Manasseh become part of the Twelve Tribes; the tribe of Joseph is represented by his two sons.

It is very puzzling that Joseph, who was the most beloved son of Jacob, as well as the son of his old age, suddenly recedes from the picture of the Twelve Tribes, replaced by his two sons, Ephraim and Manasseh. Furthermore, it has become traditional in Jewish homes, on Friday night and the eve of holidays, to bless one's children by saying, "May God make you like Ephraim and Manasseh."

Why were Jacob's grandchildren selected as an eternal blessing for all generations to come? I suggest that when a Jew recites the "Hear, O Israel" daily, or blesses a child before the Sabbath or a holiday, something symbolic is occurring. What is being represented is the fact that we are all reciting "Hear, O Israel," referring to Jacob, our father. We, who are separated from him by approximately 3,000 years, reaffirm the principle that "the Eternal, our God, the Eternal is the Unique One," thereby bridging time. We say to Jacob: "We have also *become* your children."

This understanding explains why we are known as the Children of Israel, i.e., the children of Jacob. We respond as the children of Jacob did, reaffirming the Jewish declaration of faith, "Hear, O Israel, the Eternal, our God: the Eternal is the Unique One."

The Talmud states that "Jacob, our father, has not died" (*Taanit* 5b). In emphasizing the eternal spirit of our forefather, the Talmud selects the name "Jacob," and not "Israel." Furthermore, the Talmud stresses the fact that Jacob *our father* has not died.

We all must strive to see ourselves as the children of Jacob at some point in our lives, identifying with his struggles as well as our own. Then, each of us can become an "Israel." The transformation of Jacob into Israel serves as a model for each of us. First, we recognize that "Jacob, our father, has not died." And then, we can each say, "Hear, O Israel, the Eternal, our God: the Eternal is the Unique One."

CHAPTER III

JACOB AND "HEAR, O ISRAEL"

I

INTRODUCTION

The Centrality of the "Hear, O Israel"

On Jacob's deathbed, he thinks of his grandfather, Abraham, who spread the message of monotheism to all peoples of the world. He envisions the entire history of the Jewish people and humanity, from the ancient past until the future arrival of the Messiah. Jacob gathers together all of his sons, the founders of the Twelve Tribes of Israel, and through Divine prophecy, foretells their destinies.

Jacob is well aware, however, that the past will be interpreted and the future will be experienced by what he says on his deathbed. He is worried that all the trials and tribulations of his grandfather, Abraham, and his father, Isaac, as well as his own turbulent life, may lead to disunity and divisiveness among his children, and may affect their belief in one God. Among Jacob's concerns about potential conflict among his children is the fact that he has four "firstborns" from four different wives -- Leah, Rachel, Bilhah and Zilpah. However, he is careful to recognize each child's individuality and different maturational processes as he prepares to bless them.

Jacob has already become whole (Genesis 33:18), healed from his limping, partly through his reconciliation with Esau, and partly through having attributed positive meanings to the adversities of his life, such as being deceived by Laban. But the resolution of one remaining issue would grant Jacob the ultimate meaning in his life. He yearns for the certainty that his children, the Twelve Tribes of Israel, the future of the Jewish people, will believe and experience the oneness of God that has always been with him, with his father, Isaac, and with his grandfather, Abraham.

The Midrash and Talmud state: "At the time that Jacob, our father, departed from this world, he gathered together his twelve sons and said to them: 'Perhaps there is a doubt in your heart about the existence and essence of the oneness of the Holy One Blessed Be He.' They said to him, in unison: *'Hear, Israel*, our Father, just as your heart is complete and one with the Holy One Blessed Be He, so in our hearts there is total accord that *the Eternal our God, the Eternal is One*.' Upon hearing these beautiful, true sentiments, Jacob's doubts were assuaged and he declared: 'Blessed be the Name of the Glorious Majesty of God forever and ever'" (Genesis *Rabbah* 98:3; Talmud, *Pesahim* 56a).

Based on this epic event in the lives of our Patriarchs and Matriarchs, the Jewish declaration of faith is expressed in the "Hear, O Israel." This declaration is formulated in the Torah as "Hear, O Israel, the Eternal our God, the Eternal is One" (Deuteronomy 6:4).

The centrality of the "Hear, O Israel" declaration is demonstrated in a number of ways. For example, it is the first prayer that Jewish parents teach their children, and the last prayer that a Jew recites before dying. Throughout life, Jews, old and young, recite this prayer at least twice a day, in the morning and evening, and before retiring at night.

Jacob and Jewish Belief

Jacob sees himself as the essential link between his grandfather, Abraham, who spread monotheism, and the era of the Messiah, when such knowledge and recognition will be universal. Through the continuing daily recitation of the "Hear, O Israel," Jacob is the focus not only of a core belief, but also of an ethical framework by which to live, based on monotheism.

The most striking aspect of the Midrash quoted above is that the children of Jacob addressed him in *unison*, with one voice, indicating their common understanding and belief. Furthermore, the way that they addressed their father is meaningful to us and to all succeeding generations of Jews. After they began with "Hear...," they paused and considered whether they should address their father as Jacob or Israel. The same Divine spirit came over all of the sons, as they instinctively knew what to say. They chose their father's alternate name, "Israel," representing a person who had struggled and had undergone transformation in his life. Israel's children understood their father's struggles. Perhaps even more importantly, they understood their own, ranging from sibling rivalries to searches for ultimate meaning in their individual encounters with the changing Images of God.

Similarly, all Jewish people throughout the generations continue to go through their own episodes of struggle and transformation. Our struggles in relationship to God and with our opposites and ourselves lead to the realization that we are all "Israel." What keeps us together is the belief that God is with us, as promised to our forefather, Jacob/Israel, during his dream about the Ladder of Ascension (Genesis 28:12-15).

II

The Language of the "Hear, O Israel"

The Torah's formulation of the "Hear, O Israel" (Deuteronomy 6:4) presents a number of possible interpretations.

I suggest that the "Hear, O Israel" may be understood in three different ways. One understanding is that this declaration is addressed to Jacob by his "children." That is, we continue the legacy of Jacob and address him as our father, when we declare that "the Eternal our God, the Eternal is One." This interpretation is in keeping with Jacob's words in Genesis 48:5, where Jacob "adopts" his grandchildren, Ephraim and Manasseh, by publicly accepting them on the same level as his own sons, Reuben and Simeon. We are all the descendants, or grandchildren, of Jacob, and it is, therefore, natural that we should feel like his own children in declaring the central Jewish belief that is expressed in the "Hear, O Israel." This approach may provide an added dimension to our understanding of the Rabbinical statement (Talmud, *Taanit* 5b) that Jacob, our father, has not died. He is a real presence in our daily lives, as we confirm in our declaration of belief.

A second interpretation of Deuteronomy 6:4 is that the "Hear, O Israel" is addressed by each of us to the "Israel" within each of us. Every morning and evening, together with Jews all over the world, we recite the "Hear, O Israel" to the Jewish collective whole -- from Abraham, our forefather, to future Jews who will witness the Messianic era -- as well as to each individual Jew and to our own struggling selves.

A third interpretation understands that we address the God within each of us. The internal struggle between the Divine and human aspects of our being may be alluded to in the name "Israel," which means wrestling with God.

Finally, each of us may choose to synthesize all or some of the above interpretations at the moment that we recite the "Hear, O Israel," and our personal interpretation does not have to remain static. On any given day or at any given time of day, our inclination may be to focus on an aspect of the prayer that speaks to our soul at that moment.

Before we recite the prayer, we are obligated to pause for a moment of silence, giving us an opportunity to collect our thoughts and reflect on what we are about to say, as well as what is in our minds and hearts. This self-reflection will lead to true *kavvanah* (intention), both in reciting the prayer and acting upon it. As discussed below, those who truly "hear" the words that they recite will respond by acting accordingly, in an ethical, godly fashion.

Essentially, by reciting the declaration of faith, one addresses God directly. Furthermore, by reciting the "Hear, O Israel," one accepts upon oneself the yoke of the Kingdom of Heaven (*Ol Malkhut Shamayim*), i.e., the supreme obligation of walking in God's ways.

All of the above pertains to hearing God on an individual, personal level. However, this hearing can ultimately be translated into building a collection of individuals with common perceptions and common goals -- a nation, a people. Abram's response to hearing the voice of God was to heed His words of *Lekh Lekha* (Genesis 12:1), "go forth," leaving the familiar and comfortable perceptions and surroundings of his youth. This was the necessary first step in his building a new nation. During this process, Abram became Abraham, "the father of a multitude of nations"

(Genesis 17:5), as well as the father of the Jewish people. Abraham's message of monotheism spread to the far corners of the globe, teaching a new way of understanding the human-Divine partnership.

The Words of the "Hear, O Israel"

The "Hear, O Israel" prayer consists of only six Hebrew words. In the Torah text (Deuteronomy 6:4), two of the Hebrew letters are written larger than the rest -- the *Ayin* in the word *Shema* ("Hear") and the *Dalet* in the word *Ehad* ("One"). Together these two letters spell *Ed*, meaning "witness." Our Rabbis interpret this emphasis as indicating that those who say the "Hear, O Israel" serve as witnesses from generation to generation to the truths that the living God is within each of us, there is but one God, and the God of our forefathers is also our God.

The "Hear, O Israel" is divided into two parts: "Hear, O Israel," and "the Eternal our God, the Eternal is One." The Rabbis of the Midrash analyze this division to better understand the nature of the Divine revelation at Sinai and the privilege of reciting the "Hear, O Israel." The *Midrash Rabbah* (Deuteronomy 2:31 [on 6:4]) states:

> From where does Israel have the privilege to recite the "Hear, O Israel?" Rabbi Pinhas bar Hama said, from the act of revelation at Sinai, where God Himself uttered the "Hear, O Israel." Before beginning [the Ten Commandments with] 'I am the Eternal, your God,' He called: 'Hear, O Israel,' and all affirmed: 'The Eternal our God, the Eternal is One.'"

Interestingly, after the giving of the Ten Commandments, the Children of Israel expressed their fear of continuing to hear the voice of God speaking directly to them. In Deuteronomy 5:21-24, right after the Israelites heard the Divinely revealed Ten Commandments, they said to Moses:

> ...We have *heard* His voice out of the midst of the fire...Now therefore why should we die?...if we hear the voice of the Lord our God any more, then we shall die...

God listened to their request. The placement of the "*Hear*, O Israel" following their request seems to imply that from now on God's voice will take on a different form. God will continue to speak to the people through their inner hearing of God's voice. This phenomenon will continue to be paramount in their lives and in those of all future generations.

Each word of the "Hear, O Israel" has special significance and importance. Therefore, every word of the declaration is analyzed in the section that follows.

Hear ("Shema")

The central declaration of Jewish faith is directed to our sense of hearing. This formulation is not surprising in view of the fact that it was through *hearing* the voice of God at Sinai that the Israelites unconditionally accepted the One God and His Torah. Throughout Jewish history, that voice has continued to resonate within each Jew -- the voice that is the basis for belief and for action. Our Rabbis expound on the fact that hearing is more powerful than seeing as a basis for faith. It is easier to *imagine* something infinite through the sense of hearing than through other senses, such as vision or touch, that are bound by finite dimensions. Furthermore, hearing leads to belief. One can perceive and touch idols, but one cannot hear them speak.

Rabbi Dr. Adolf (Avraham) Altmann, former Chief Rabbi of Trier, Germany, masterfully examines the imperative of continuing to hear the voice of God on a daily basis. He explores the central role of hearing during the revelation at Sinai and throughout Jewish history in his analysis of the "Hear, O Israel" (A. Altmann, 1928, 1991):

> God's Sinai voice has never turned silent for us; its echo continues throughout time. Only through this continued, inner, intuitive receptivity to that Divine voice has Israel's belief in God remained...
> (p. 61)

Furthermore, as Rabbi Altmann points out, the ability to hear the Divine voice is directly related to action and to ethics.

> The universe is filled with voices, but only those attuned will hear them...God's voice of revelation cannot have become audible only once for all time...If the Jew applies his heart to things that concern faith and that concern life, if he inclines his inner ear with its specific sensitivity, he will hear the voices. How can one direct the inner ear above all foreign outside noise toward the ancient voice calling from Sinai? The answer is, with the heart. (p. 65)

In other words, the ear must hear the language of the lips when the "Hear, O Israel" is recited. Then, the actions of the individual must follow this Divine call to act justly. If one hears the call from Sinai and its quiet, daily echoes, one is obligated to act on that Divine message, in a godly, ethical fashion.

> There are voices and calls which sound out loud, yet one fails to hear them, and there are others that make no sound at all, yet they are heard. The human without ethics passes by what cries out most in life without hearing, whereas one of high moral character hears even the most subdued call and traces its source...If no one else hears the silent cry of the humiliated, the powerless, hidden victims, the Jew must hear it; that is the noblest ethical significance of the "Hear, O Israel." (p. 63)

Israel ("Yisrael")

The second word of the central declaration of Jewish faith is "Israel." This brings to mind Jacob's pivotal encounter that led to his receiving an alternate name -- Israel.

Genesis 32:25-33 presents an account of Jacob's encounter with an *Ish* (an angel, a human being as a messenger of God, or an internal struggle) and his acquisition of the name "Israel." That episode of struggle and wrestling may be understood as Jacob's *lonely night journey*. The experience of going through such a "dark night of the soul" is one which all must undertake if they wish to achieve the goal of realizing their creative potential. Everyone goes through such a journey in life; not once, but many times.

In the Biblical story concerning Jacob, the name "Israel" is explained as follows: "And the *Ish* said: 'Jacob shall not be your exclusive name; you will also be known as Israel, because you have prevailed with God and with men'" (Genesis 32:29).

Each person who recites the "Hear, O Israel" may be engaging in a type of soliloquy, or dialogue with the self. Life presents itself in a manner whereby individuals have frequent, ongoing struggles -- with God, with the Image of God and with humans. Thus, this monologue-prayer may be, in one sense, addressed to the God within. The Divine promise is that individuals will prevail in their struggles and give birth to "new" selves, of greater dimensions, as a result of these difficulties. The key word in the Biblical account is *va-tukhal*, "and you have prevailed." By working through periods of difficulty and finding meaning and growth through this process, one may attain a higher stage of existence and understanding.

Life presents individuals with the opportunity to pass through sequential stages and achieve continued growth. However, life often presents numerous difficulties in terms of relationships -- with individuals, families, business partners, communities, societies and nations, as well as with God. Even on his deathbed, Jacob faced a new struggle as he wondered whether his children would continue in the way that he had directed them.

Jacob's struggles are significant in serving as examples for each person's life journey. The meaning of the ebbs and flows that we encounter in life experiences is sometimes easy to grasp and sometimes totally hidden from us. As a result, we are alternately angry, frustrated, depressed or elated.

Sometimes a difficult encounter allows us to resolve issues from our distant past. For example, we may have had difficulties with our parents that were never resolved. Yet, at a later stage in life, we may meet other individuals who share some of our parents' characteristics and qualities. By relating to these new people in our life, we may ultimately be able to work out difficulties that date back to our childhood, thereby achieving self-realization and individuation. Furthermore, by repairing our relationships with our parents, we may find new paths and directions in our approaches to God, since the image we have of God is partially based on our relationships with our parents.

Healing and the Higher Self

This entire process of continuing encounter, struggle, new understanding and personal growth leads to living life on an increasingly elevated plane. One can move from one plateau to another throughout life. This experience is the true meaning of "healing." Whatever happens in life can be used to heal relationships with people and with God.

In this way, through this process, one experiences growth and learns how to get in touch with one's Higher Self. This concept means achieving the ability to transcend the ordinary and to imbue the ordinary with meaning and spirituality.

In thinking about Jacob's struggle and his subsequent rebirth as Israel, one is also reminded that this struggle took place at *night*, a time that gives rise to dreams and other manifestations of the unconscious. In his commentary on this Biblical episode, Maimonides (*Guide of the Perplexed* 2:43) alludes to the possibility that Jacob's encounter with the *Ish* may have been some sort of vision that occurred while Jacob was in an altered state of consciousness.

Based on Jacob's visions during that night of struggle, Jacob might have been pleased to realize that the Jewish people to follow him would also pay careful attention to the interpretation of dreams and visions. Dreams and other aspects of the unconscious form part of God's forgotten language that Jews continue to use to explore both internal and external conflicts.

The printed text of the Torah includes notations to indicate how each word is to be chanted. After the initial reflective soliloquy of "Hear, O Israel," the text indicates that one should pause. Perhaps this is a reminder that after each "Israel," i.e. after each internal and external struggle, one should try to assimilate the knowledge gained from the experience and the new perspectives before proceeding to the next stage of life.

As discussed above, when one recites the "Hear, O Israel," one also addresses each individual Jew and the collective Jewish people, from earliest times to the distant future. Furthermore, the "Hear, O Israel" serves as the last statement of a Jewish person facing immediate death. Commenting on this role of the prayer, Dr. Erwin (Morenu Shlomo Bunim) Altman, one of the sons of Rabbi Adolf (Avraham) Altmann, presented his own living testimony and analysis a short time before his own death (E. Altman, 1988):

> As the Five Books of Moses, which contain the godly testimony of His holy life, end with the words: *Le'ene Kol Yisrael*, "before the eyes of all Israel," so a Jewish *Tzaddik* and every righteous person dies before the eyes of all his people, communicating with them in his last star-hour message. Even in death he thinks more of the people he is leaving behind than of himself. And he passes from this world with an entirely selfless fulfillment of a *Mitzvah*: comforting, encouraging, uplifting and inspiring the godly people of "Aloneness," his fellow *Bney Israel* - "*Shema Yisrael*!" (p. 162)

III

The second part of the "Hear, O Israel" is "the Eternal, our God, the Eternal is One." This affirmation is equivalent to the *na'aseh ve-nishma* ("we shall do and we shall hear") declaration of the Jewish people at Sinai (Exodus 24:7), when they received the Torah. Therefore, Jews recite daily not only a confirmation and reaffirmation of monotheism, but also an acceptance of "we shall do and we shall hear."

In this declaration of acceptance, equal emphasis is placed on doing and on hearing. "Doing" is the acceptance of the rituals. But the "hearing" is equally significant. It means not only understanding the meaning of the rituals, but also continuing to hear the voice of God throughout one's life.

The practice of the *mitzvot* (commandments) heightens our awareness and sensitivities, imbuing ordinary events with spirituality and holiness. This is the underlying philosophy of the *mitzvot*. The ordinary daily routines of men, women, children, the old and the young, involve activities that are needed to maintain, preserve and enhance life. Yet, all of these activities can be raised to a level of *kedushah* (holiness). Thus, Jewish commandments, practices and customs are not distinct from the ordinary, daily life of the person, family or community. The *mitzvot* take those things that are necessary to sustain life and imbue them with holiness and transcendence.

The Eternal (pronounced "Adonai," written YHWH)

"The Eternal" refers to the quintessential nature of the existence and essence of God. This Name connotes that God's time frame is unique -- God was, is and will be. For God, these three aspects of time coexist simultaneously, rather than following one another in linear fashion. For a human being, this concept is incomprehensible, underscoring the mysterious, unfathomable essence of God.

In contradistinction, humanity lives in the present, reflects upon the past, and anticipates the future. But God's essence combines all times. When we acknowledge the Eternal, we imagine ourselves experiencing the Divine revelation, standing at Mount Sinai, accepting the Torah and hearing the voice of God. We reaffirm that acceptance for present and future generations.

Although this Name of God, the Eternal, is mentioned in the Book of Genesis, it is first explained in Exodus (3:14). There, God said to Moses: "I AM THAT I AM," following Moses's experiencing the Divine Presence in the burning bush that was not consumed. The word "Eternal" signifies that God will always be with the Jewish people. This is very similar to what God told Jacob, i.e., "I will not abandon you" (Genesis 28:15).

It is significant that the meaning of "Eternal" is given after the episode of the burning bush. That encounter signifies to all future generations that God's Eternal Presence needs to be experienced in everyone's own life -- daily, weekly or yearly -- in different ways. When God calls unto Moses, he responds with one Hebrew word, *Hineni* (Exodus 3:4), meaning "here I am." Those reading about this encounter get the feeling that someone who experiences the Divine responds with a sense of acceptance and surrender in the awesome Presence of the Divine.

The human response seems to be: "I am Your obedient servant. I am grateful to be able to experience this aspect of life. I will go in the way that You direct me. I will carry this experience with me forever. I will bring it into other parts of my daily life in order to experience new forms of 'God's Presence in the burning bush.'" Although we recognize that our earthly existence is temporal, every person can connect with the eternal Presence of God in a spiritual manner.

The Name of the Eternal Being is now pronounced "Adonai," meaning "My Master," indicating that we are the obedient servants of the will of God. We do not know the original pronunciation of this Name. However, we do know that this Name has so much sanctity that it was uttered only once a year, by the High Priest, on the Day of Atonement in the Temple's Holy of Holies. These limitations add an additional element of mystery to this supreme Name of God. The unfathomable mystery of the existence and essence of God, "I AM THAT I AM," is something that every individual grapples with throughout his or her life in personal, unique ways.

E. Altman brought new meaning to the first message that God gave to Abraham as he undertook his lifelong task of spreading monotheism, *Veheyeh Berakhah*, "And be a blessing" (Genesis 12:2). Altman pointed out that the same four Hebrew letters of "be" (WHYH) are identical with those that make up the Name of the Eternal (YHWH), though they are arranged in a slightly different order. Thus, the ethical imperative of monotheistic belief is related to embodying the highest goal of human action, i.e., being a blessing.

E. Altman expounded on this similarity between the letters of God's Name (YHWH) and "And be (WHYH) a blessing." In his amplification of this idea, he writes:

> Man's destiny to "Be a Blessing" can be conceived on various levels. It proclaims the constructive principle against any destructive tendencies. It means love in thought, words and action. But it has deeper dimensions..."And Be a Blessing"...addresses man's higher self, saying: by your faith and fulfillment of God's call, "Be a Blessing," you reach a stage of understanding of its highest spiritual meaning: *Veheyeh* - you are that you were, you are that you are,

you are that you shall be -- a continuous potential source of blessing, as you are an eternal 'partner' within God's love and His eternity. (p. 146-7)

E. Altman emphasizes that this message is addressed to Abraham and "to each individual in each generation, as each is created in the Image of God, which is a basic Biblical concept."

This understanding explains the relationship between monotheism and ethics in daily life. When one acts ethically, others notice and respond accordingly. Furthermore, they want to know the basis for the ethical behavior. What is its origin? What is the source of these absolute standards of justice, honesty and goodness? By living up to these elevated standards of behavior, individual Jews can fulfill their ultimate mission of being a "kingdom of priests and a holy nation" (Exodus 19:6), as well as a "light unto the nations" (Isaiah 60:3).

Our God ("Elohenu")

As we proceed through life, we experience multiple Images of God, even though we are aware that God is an Eternal Presence. These multiple Images explain why the Torah utilizes several different Names for God. *Elohenu* is the combined form of *Elohim shelanu*, "our God." This Name includes the concept of God as not only an Eternal Presence, but also as a judge. That the word *elohim* means "judges" is clearly indicated in Exodus 21:6. Thus, we acknowledge that God has given us a moral standard to live up to.

This Image of God as Judge indicates that He yearns for His people to live up to standards which are beneficial *for them*. Hence, we are told "to keep *for thy good* the commandments of the Lord and His statutes..." (Deuteronomy 10:13). Even when God is experienced as the God not only of love, but also of judgment, we recognize that the judgment is based on love, and its goal is to help the individual and the nation.

The term *Elohenu*, "our God," has additional meaning for us. It implies that the God of Abraham, Isaac, Jacob and Moses -- the One each experienced during his life -- is also the God who leads each of us in our life's journey. While we accept the special relationships that are forefathers enjoyed with God, nevertheless we have to personalize our own Image of God. Our life journeys are just as significant as those of our forebears. Ultimately, we must recognize that during our lives -- at high points and low points -- God is with us, just as He was with our forefathers.

The Eternal (pronounced "Adonai," written YHWH)

It seems unusual that this Name appears a second time in the very brief "Hear, O Israel." One explanation is that this repetition differentiates between a transcendent, external, incomprehensible God and an immanent, accessible, personal God.

The first time that the Eternal's Name appears, it refers to the transcendent God of history, such as the Image that appeared to Moses at the burning bush. However, after we recite the *Elohenu*, we personalize and accept *our* own Images of God. We thus experience God on a personal level and find our own Eternal -- Who was, is and will be with each of us.

Ehad ("One")

The Oneness of the God of Israel is a recurring theme in the Torah. The best known source of this essential Jewish belief is the first two commandments of the Decalogue, which are echoed in the "Hear, O Israel" (Exodus 20:2-3). As discussed above, each of us encounters multiple Images of God during our lives, just as our forebears did. However, all of these are manifestations of the One God, Who appeared to Abraham, Isaac, Jacob, Moses, Sarah, Rebekah, Rachel, Leah, etc. For example, when God appears to Jacob during his dream about the Ladder of Ascension, God identifies Himself to Jacob as "the God of Abraham, thy father, and the God of Isaac" (Genesis 28:13).

The concept of One God is fundamental to the ethical framework of the Jewish people. Only One God who is immutable can give one set of everlasting values, principles and standards by which individuals and a nation are to live. These standards are not subject to variation or to change, as they may be in polytheistic societies.

Furthermore, E. Altman (1988) relates the concept of the One to aloneness, and thus to reciting the "Hear, O Israel" at the end of life. He writes:

> [The "Hear, O Israel"] has many equally valid interpretations and translations, but the recitation and proclamation of the *Shema* at the very moment of death is probably meant in the sense: *Adonay* is our God from without and within, *Adonay* alone! This testimony reflects the most intimate direct relationship with God; man feels and realizes: I am dying alone, as nobody can accompany me, where I am going. I am "on my own," as never before in my life, but just in this "alone-ness," which I am facing now, I am closer to God's identity and His Alone-ness than ever before. In this true alone-ness, I experience and recognize my very own Divinity from within in the Image of God. (p. 161)

In addition to this "identification" with the Divine, I find great personal comfort in the Image of Divine Oneness. This concept reflects the oneness that pervades much of life. Every day, I am aware of the oneness of humanity -- the similar drives, fears, hopes, dreams and aspirations that we all share. We share one space, the earth, on which we strive to make a difference for the short spans of our individual lives. We share the same spiritual quests, which although they take us along different paths, lead us to answers that we seek to universal questions. This awareness of oneness -- that of the human experience of the cosmos and the universal pursuit of religious experience -- can enhance our daily encounters with other individuals, communities and nations, thereby enriching our lives.

On a personal level, the recitation of the "Hear, O Israel" allows us to listen to our inner voice, thus guiding us in achieving our highest potential and becoming our best selves. "This ability to listen and to hear allows the voice of God to be heard continually on a daily basis. This is a central aspect of individuation" (Meier, 1991).

Every prayer must be recited with intention and with some level of understanding of what is uttered. However, the recitation of the "Hear, O Israel" requires a particularly deep understanding that emanates from one's heart and soul. The Sages placed the recitation of the "Hear, O Israel" in a class above the other commandments. They mandated that this prayer should be recited with particular "intention of the heart" (Talmud, *Berakhot* 13a-b). Therefore, one should recite the "Hear, O Israel" with particular concentration on each word and concept contained therein.

Another unique feature of this prayer's recitation is the custom of prolonging the sounding of the large letter *Dalet* at the end of the word *Ehad* ("One"). The prolongation of this sound heightens one's awareness of the other large letter in the prayer, the *Ayin* at the end of *Shema* ("Hear"). As discussed above, these two letters form the word *Ed*, "witness."

When we recite the "Hear, O Israel" with this level of intention and attention, we indeed become witnesses, bearing personal testimony to the historical revelation at Sinai and to the ongoing revelation that each of us can achieve in our daily lives. Furthermore, we become witnesses to the fact that each of us is a link in the long chain of tradition, enhancing the meaning of our own lives, and passing on our personal testimony and our own spirituality to this generation, as well as the next.

SHEMA, YISRAEL, ADONAI ELOHENU, ADONAI EHAD!
Hear, O Israel, the Eternal our God, the Eternal is One!

CHAPTER IV

AS JACOB IS TOUCHED BY HIS FATHER

I

INTRODUCTION

Jacob is scared and trembles as he begins to share publicly what his early childhood was like with respect to what his soul experienced -- particularly, his relationship with his father and mother, his experience of his parents' marriage, and his relationship with his twin older brother, Esau.

It is well known and even explicitly mentioned that Isaac loved his son Esau because he always honored Isaac with delicious food brought back from his hunting expeditions. It is also known that the twins' mother, Rebekah, loved and favored Jacob (Genesis 25:28).

Even though Jacob had his mother's love, at times he felt like an abandoned child because he passionately yearned for his father's love. But his father did not play with him, did not cuddle him as an infant or child. No one knew this, and Jacob could not tell anyone about it. After all, everyone thought they knew Isaac, the great pious Jewish Patriarch. He had received blessings from his father, Abraham. Furthermore, the covenantal promise given by God to Abraham was transmitted to Isaac.

Oh, Isaac did talk to Jacob. He told his son several times and reiterated on every occasion possible how his life was spared in that monumental Biblical historical epoch known as "The Binding of Isaac." That was all he could talk about. He was obsessed with this episode. He shared with Jacob the observation that even though his life was spared, he subsequently had a hard time trusting other people. Remember that his own father, Abraham, had approached him and asked him to go for a walk. That simple walk led to his being bound on an altar. Even though Isaac's life was spared, the news of the near tragedy affected his mother, Sarah, to such an extent that she died instantly, probably from shock (Midrash *Rabbah*, Leviticus 20:2).

Isaac never stopped talking about the binding episode. He went on and on, and as he reflected on the event, he felt enormously guilty at being part of the overall experience. He seemed to feel that Abraham's withholding the news of "The Binding of Isaac" from his wife, giving her no prior warning, was probably a primary factor in Sarah's sudden death.

Jacob listened to Isaac, but his self-absorption caused Jacob to feel unloved, perhaps even unworthy of love. Isaac never touched Jacob, talked to Jacob or even walked with him. Jacob understood his father's obsession with the "Binding of Isaac." His binding created constant flashbacks for him and therefore he never wanted to take simple walks with Jacob. But understanding Isaac's obsessive pathology did not alleviate the enormously painful and fearful experience of Jacob's not receiving paternal love.

It is written of Jacob, "And Jacob was a whole person dwelling in tents" (Genesis 25:27). This indeed sounds exquisite. But that was only his external persona. He was tormented internally. He felt unloved by his father. Of course, he empathized with his father's plight, but his internal, essential needs were unfulfilled.

Jacob's pain was exacerbated when Esau brought food for Isaac and in turn, received lavish praise for his strength and vitality. Jacob, this "whole person dwelling in tents," cried internally and was perplexed with his family dynamics, which obviously also colored his perception of the world at large.

Jacob's childhood was not entirely bleak. His mother genuinely loved him. That he felt to his core. But even in this love there was pain, because the love was always given privately, when Jacob's father was not around. His mother was so sweet and tender, but Jacob wondered if she was secretly afraid of her husband's opinions and even more afraid of his temper. They seemed relatively happily married, but Jacob sensed that his parents each had a distinct and separate life which they did not share with one another. In his studies, Jacob remembered the ideal of marriage as expressed in the Bible: "A husband shall cleave to his wife and they shall become one flesh" (Genesis 2:24). But the reality Jacob experienced in his home was that his parents cleaved together, yet remained two *conflicted* individuals. For example, his mother spoke directly to his father only once (Genesis 27:46), when she told him that Jacob was going away from home to look for a wife. And even this one communication was less than honest. Jacob was really leaving home because his brother Esau's rage was uncontrollable and he would have murdered Jacob.

Although the Torah was revealed to the collective Jewish people at Mount Sinai, all the Patriarchs and Matriarchs studied the concepts of the Torah through individual Divine prophecy (Midrash, Genesis *Rabbah* 26:5). During Jacob's childhood, he studied the Torah and the mysteries of life. He had a complete understanding of natural law and the lives of animals and trees. But he never experienced a complete inner peace. He did not know which forces governed his own life. However, Jacob knew deep down in his soul that love is as essential to life as any biological need. Jacob knew *his mission* in the development of his own life was to try to achieve paternal love and the domestic tranquility that was missing in his childhood, these being central to one's well-being.

This mission was the secret agenda of Jacob's life -- to feel whole, to feel loved, to seek security not only in theoretical study, but in living life with his father, his mother, his brother and later, with his own family. Jacob wanted to have a complete understanding of the marital dynamics that he experienced in his family.

Please do not misunderstand this analysis of Jacob's inner life. He was not physically or sexually abused. His father was not an alcoholic. His parents were faithful to one another and were financially secure. None of these issues was ever a concern. Nevertheless, his family was what is usually described as dysfunctional. A dysfunctional family is never determined by measures of external abuse, but rather on the basis of the internal experience of each family member.

Jacob, "the whole person dwelling in tents," was emotionally scarred and abused. When he tried to speak to his father, Isaac was not there for him. Jacob developed an ulcer, right in the core of his being. This was not an ulcer that could be cured through an endoscopic procedure, but an ulcer, a hole, a vacuum, that extended right down to his existential core.

His mother's love was tainted by its privacy and secrecy. His brother, Esau, was his opposite. Maybe Jacob should have been able to appreciate the warrior archetype that Esau represented, but Jacob's studies of the Torah certainly discouraged and disparaged the hunter-warrior archetype.

Jacob's mission in life was to become aware of his own internal vacuum and to use this challenge in the most constructive way possible for himself, and in keeping with what he knew must be a Divine plan. Ultimately, this is the mandate for every human being: to be aware of one's own frailties, vulnerabilities and humanity and to use this realization to become whole and a partner with God. Thus, throughout life, each person develops a changing personal relationship with God. We can thus inspire and enhance all of God's creations and allow ourselves to feel loved and healed, thereby becoming truly "whole."

II

BEING TOUCHED AND RECEIVING THE BLESSING

As Isaac aged, his eyesight diminished significantly (Genesis 27:1). He could not recognize his sons. Since he was unable to identify them with his eyes, he was forced to use his other senses. He recognized Jacob and Esau by their voices, their manner of speaking, and by touching them. His diminishing eyesight did not surprise Jacob. Jacob even anticipated it, because Isaac's vision was always poor; not in the literal sense, but in his judgment in family matters and interpersonal family dynamics.

Towards the end of his life, Isaac was ready to bestow his paternal blessing upon Esau. Rebekah knew of his intention, and she decided, based on Divine prophecy (Genesis 6:23) that Jacob, the younger child, was destined to receive this special ancestral blessing. She told Jacob to dress up like Esau, use a ruse to imitate his hairy skin and go hunting. Then Jacob was to bring the food to Isaac before Esau could bring his catch, so that the prophecy she received before the twins' birth would be fulfilled, and Jacob would receive the special blessing from his father.

Jacob was very hesitant to implement his mother's directive. She told him about the prophecy, but he wondered why his father had not received the same prophecy, or why his mother did not share this essential prophecy with his father.

Jacob was afraid that his imitating Esau would create more enmity between his father and himself. If Isaac discovered that Jacob had deceived him, would he be cast out of his father's house, just as his uncle, Ishmael, was cast out of Abraham's house based on the advice of Sarah, Jacob's grandmother? Would this family pattern be repeated?

But most of all, Jacob was afraid to actually go hunting. Could a "man who is whole and dwells in tents" go hunting? Is he strong enough? Jacob was now asked to do that which he most despised about his brother. Was Jacob up to the task? He felt weak and inadequate. He knew that he excelled in studies and penetrating the mysteries of the world, but could he shoot an animal with a bow and arrow?

Jacob decided to try. As he ambivalently started his adventure in order to receive the ancestral blessing, he borrowed his brother's bow and arrow. He had a terrible flashback of how he had stolen the birthright years before, when Esau came home tired and worn out. Jacob took advantage of his brother's weariness then. What was he doing now?

Was this the way to receive the ancestral blessings? Is the road to self-fulfillment paved with deceptive motives and actions?

To Jacob's utter surprise, he was successful in his hunting expedition. He could not explain it because he hated hunting. However, it was not as bad as he had anticipated. Now he seemed to look at Esau differently. What Jacob had really despised was his own lack of strength. He was envious of Esau's strength. Now Jacob had discovered his own strength. God was really with him.

His mother continued to assist Jacob in this ruse. She suggested that he take two goats from the family's flock, so that she could quickly prepare a tasty dish for Isaac.

When Jacob delivered the food to his father, Isaac was surprised at how quickly the food had been prepared, and he asked Jacob about it. Jacob responded not as Esau, but as "the whole man dwelling in tents," saying "God assisted me in the preparation" (Genesis 27:20). When Jacob mentioned the word "God," his father questioned whether the son before him was Esau or Jacob. The success in hunting was typical of Esau, while the word "God" was typical of Jacob.

Isaac's eyesight was poor. He asked Jacob to approach him, so that he could touch his son and determine whether it was Esau, the hairy one, or Jacob, the whole man dwelling in tents.

Isaac touched Jacob and proclaimed that the voice was the voice of Jacob, while the hands were the hands of Esau (Genesis 27:20). Isaac was correct. Jacob had integrated divinity, the mentioning of God, and the human experience of hunting into one. Jacob was becoming whole. The process had begun.

But more important was the "touch." Jacob could not believe the experience. Tears ran down his cheeks, and his heart melted as he felt the loving touch of his father for the first time in his life. Jacob totally surrendered to the moment. It did not matter that Isaac thought he was Esau, because in that moment Jacob possessed the Esau characteristics of strength and vitality, intertwined with his own persona of the whole man dwelling in tents.

His father's touch was the turning point of Jacob's life. He knew it would endure for the rest of his days. He felt blessed. Jacob did not even remember the content of his father's blessing, but he would never forget the experience of feeling touched lovingly by his father. He was now strong. He was the best of Esau and the best of Jacob - all put together in one. He was beginning to feel truly whole.

III

THE PROMISE OF GOD'S PROTECTION

Jacob was not sure how his life would begin to develop after the process of integrating his soul and body began. He felt different. He felt more resilient. The same things that he had perceived as impediments and obstacles in his former way of life now became objects of endearment. A bow and arrow, the act of hunting animals, and nature all took on special significance for him. He was able to perceive animation in objects that previously seemed totally inanimate.

Despite this inner transformation, he followed his mother's advice and fled Be'er Sheva in order to avoid Esau's wrath and vengeance. As he was leaving on his way to Haran, night approached and he felt tired and scared. Spontaneously, he prayed to God that his new strength, his new wholeness, would stay with him in his new circumstances. He suddenly felt a tiredness descend upon him and he needed to go to sleep. For the first time, he rested upon the earth. He found a rock that looked very special, so he used it as a pillow.

Jacob admitted to himself that he still harbored doubts as to whether he would fall asleep. After all, he always fell asleep in his tent, resting on comfortable pillows, but how would he manage with a rock?

That night, his sleep and his dream were the best of his entire life. His dream has become known as the one dealing with the "Ladder of Ascension," where angels of God ascend and descend from earth all the way to heaven. God promised Jacob that He would always be with him.

Jacob was elated. His dream suggested two ultimate meta-communications. First, he had not only integrated strength and vitality with the whole man dwelling in tents, but this integration had enhanced his life, his dreams, his aspirations and inspirations. The angels ascending and descending represented very strong figures, able to go all the way from earth to heaven.

Second, he had received a promise of personal protection by God. The presence of God would be with him for the rest of his life. As a result of that promise, Jacob's "heart lifted up his feet and it was easy to walk" (Midrash *Rabbah*, Genesis 29:1). His motivation and zest for life would be intertwined with knowing and feeling the presence of God, even during times of trial and tribulation.

IV

AS ESAU HUGGED JACOB

Later, after Jacob's struggle during a different night journey and his name change to Israel (Genesis 32:25-33), he felt more confident about meeting his brother Esau again, desperately hoping for a brotherly reconciliation.

When Esau saw Jacob, he witnessed a new person. He saw his own characteristics mirrored in Jacob. He saw Jacob not as a weak brother who deceived and tricked, but as a strong man, integrating the best of each of the twins to form a whole, complete person.

Esau also noticed that Jacob was limping, which indicated to him that Jacob had struggled emotionally and physically to become who he was. Esau felt there was no longer a need to continue the sibling rivalry. Esau ran to meet the "new" Jacob, and he hugged him and kissed him on the neck.

Jacob was in shock. He had never before been genuinely and affectionately touched by his brother. He felt this touch as further healing for having been unloved by his father.

First his father had touched him, and now his brother. God was really with him. He felt alive, happy and full of life. His lifelong wounds were slowly being healed. He felt invigorated and full of renewed strength, spiritual and physical.

Opposites were united. Reconciliation had occurred. Angels had ascended from earth to heaven. A hunter and whole man dwelling in tents had touched each other. Differences were recognized and respected. Envy and hatred were transformed into heightened self-awareness and an inner peacefulness for both Esau and Jacob. They recognized that no family situation or circumstance stays the same forever. People and circumstances change, attitudes are reformed and reconciliations are possible.

V

ESAU AND JACOB BURY THEIR FATHER, ISAAC

Isaac died at a ripe old age of 180 and both of his sons, Esau and Jacob, buried their father in Kiryat Arba, in the same place where Abraham, their grandfather, was buried (Genesis 35:29).

Esau and Jacob had already reconciled with one another. Jacob was also healed from his mystical encounter with the *Ish*, an angel (Genesis 33:18).

Together they stood, side by side, tearful, as their father was laid to rest. Esau, the older brother, the son who was exemplary in honoring his father, was the first to put earth on his father's coffin. At that moment, Jacob, who was now healed, discovered a new insight. Everyone has positive and negative attributes and characteristics. Esau may not have been a whole man dwelling in tents, but neither was Jacob. Everyone develops throughout life. Jacob did not need to be angry or jealous concerning the characteristics of Esau which he lacked, because he had acquired new internal strength of his own. The second shovel of earth was put on Isaac's coffin by Jacob, and the third was put on by both Esau and Jacob, as a sign of oneness, completeness and reconciliation.

Neither son moved after the burial. Instead they spoke to each other, really spoke to each other, perhaps for the first time in their lives. They reminisced painfully and tearfully about their follies, weaknesses and the roles each had played in their enmeshed family situation. They looked deeply into each other's eyes and noticed how they each completed and complemented one another. Jacob marvelled at the ease with which Esau had revered and honored his parents, while Esau had always taken note of how diligently Jacob studied Torah for most of the day and night. Although Jacob was not a hunter and did not like the sport of killing animals, he recognized Esau's strength and vitality, earthiness and appreciation of nature, characteristics that Jacob needed to develop throughout his life. Esau had always noted how close Jacob was to their mother, Rebekah. He envied that special ability of relating to a mother which he lacked. Indeed, the two brothers were one. They were two sides of one person who took on two separate identities.

They both expressed a private hope that future generations of Torah students would emphasize their reconciliation and ultimate union with one another, rather than their early years of turmoil, agony and deception. They prayed at their father's grave that each person would recognize the Esau and Jacob attributes within himself or herself, that each person has strengths and weaknesses, and that each person faces internal struggles.

At their father's grave Jacob and Esau embraced one another and became one.

VI

AS JACOB BLESSES HIS GRANDCHILDREN

Just as Isaac's eyesight had diminished significantly prior to his bestowing blessings on Jacob and Esau, so, too, did Jacob's eyesight diminish prior to his bestowing blessings on his grandchildren, Menasheh and Ephraim. Jacob's blessings were ultimately meant for all the generations to come.

Interestingly, the Bible uses the same root of the verb to describe Jacob's approach to Isaac, as it does for Menasheh and Ephraim's approach to Jacob -- *G'shah*, spelled Gimmel, Shin, Hay (Genesis 27:21-22 and 48:10). The verb also appears in Genesis 45:4 to describe how Joseph's brothers approach Joseph. This word suggests closeness or proximity, not only in resonance of thought which is essential, but also in physical, bodily closeness through touch, embrace and kissing.

In the depth of his heart, Jacob recalls how he received the blessing from his father, Isaac. The similarities are striking. Isaac and Jacob both had diminished eyesight. Isaac blesses two children, Jacob and Esau, and in turn, Jacob blesses two grandchildren, Ephraim and Menasheh, who are as dear to him as his own children. Both Isaac and Jacob initially bless the younger and then the older, and before the blessing, Isaac touches Jacob, and Jacob touches both his grandchildren. Patterns within families tend to be repetitive, although with slight variations. Jacob wants to bless not only Menasheh and Ephraim, but also all future children who will be born into his family.

Even before Jacob bestowed the blessings on his two grandchildren, he kissed and embraced them. This is the essential aspect before bestowing a spiritual blessing. What Jacob lacked as a child and as a young adult from his father, Isaac -- the touch, the embrace, the kiss -- he made sure to give to his grandchildren. He knew that no blessing, no words, no inspiration, no vision can ever take place without a loving touch.

Jacob told his beloved son, Joseph, that Joseph's children, his grandchildren, were as dear to him as his own children (Genesis 48:5). This beautiful message can be understood on at least two distinct levels. Jacob was still mourning the loss of his cherished wife, Rachel. Joseph greatly reminded him of his wife because of their similar characteristics and appearances. The Bible describes Rachel as *Yefat Toar V'yfat Mareh* (Genesis 29:17) and Joseph in identical language (Genesis 39:6). They were both beautiful, internally and externally. Jacob's love for his wife, Rachel, was transferred to Joseph, and through Joseph to his two grandchildren, Menasheh and Ephraim. By saying that Menasheh and Ephraim were as dear to him as Reuben and Simon (Jacob's biological firstborn), Jacob elevated the status of Joseph to that of his firstborn son. Thus, Joseph, the dreamer, the man with visions, was transformed into the firstborn son and therefore he received a double portion of the Twelve Tribes' inheritance of the Land -- one for Menasheh and one for Ephraim. This goal explains Jacob's reference to Reuben and Simon, because they were the children who were born to him first, through Leah.

So the first message of this episode for all generations is that the firstborn of a family is not necessarily the oldest of the family, but rather the visionary of the family, not the one who sees things in a concrete way, but in a way which is always inspired by Divine vision.

All of Genesis conveys a similar message that the firstborn is defined by an integration of spirituality and real life. God selected the sacrifice of Abel, but not that of Cain. Abraham's son Isaac was selected to continue the family blessing, not Ishmael. Jacob received the blessing from Isaac, not Esau. Joseph, not Reuben, received the special blessing.

The second message for all generations is found in Jacob's declaration that his grandchildren are as dear to him as his own children. Jacob is addressing all generations to come, the entire Jewish people from his time until the arrival of the Messiah, stating that all of us, his great-grandchildren, and his great-great-grandchildren are as dear to him as his own children.

When Jacob blesses his grandchildren by crossing his hands, putting his right hand on Ephraim and his left hand on Menasheh, he accentuates that the firstborn is not determined by chronological order but by one's spiritual vision. Becoming the firstborn is open and available to everyone. When Jacob touches Ephraim and Menasheh by placing his hands on top of their heads and saying the immortal words, "May God make you as Ephraim and Menasheh," he illustrates the potential for anyone and everyone to receive the blessings of the firstborn.

Thus, in every Jewish home, when a father and mother bless their children by placing their hands on the children's heads, kissing them and embracing them, each child feels the love of his or her father and mother, as well as the mystical touch of Jacob, our Patriarch. The Patriarch Jacob, who was not touched by his father as a child or young adult, touches all future generations with love, devotion and piety, thereby adopting each one of us as his children across the historical span of all the generations.

The unbelievably horrendous message that Jacob wants to convey is the recognition that every family, just as his own, will have dysfunctional aspects to it because of the wounded psyches of the mother and father.

Each child feels somewhat insecure, somewhat inadequate, and not sufficiently loved because of some painful aspect of the family. Jacob's message is that in order to arrive at the time of the ultimate redemption, each person must take his or her individual pain and transform it into a blessing for the sake of the self, children, grandchildren and all future generations. In summary, it is apparent that a central message in the entire book of Genesis is a deep understanding of what it means to be a firstborn.

- The first story of siblings is the story of Cain and Abel, where God selects the spiritual offering of the younger brother (Genesis 4:1-5).

- Isaac, the younger brother, receives the special ancestral blessing from Abraham, while Ishmael receives a blessing that he will become a great nation (Genesis 21:12-14).

- Jacob, the younger brother, receives the special blessing from his father, Isaac, while Esau is told that his descendants will become a mighty nation (Genesis 27, 25:23).

- Joseph and his two children, Ephraim and Menasheh, receive the special paternal blessing, while Reuben, the chronological firstborn, does not (Genesis 48:19, 49:3).

- Finally, Jacob blesses Ephraim with his right hand and Menasheh, the firstborn, with his left hand, indicating that "the younger brother shall be greater than he . . ." (Genesis 48:19).

A central message of the entire Book of Genesis is a redefinition of the status and definition of the firstborn.

It is very clear what it does *not* mean. It does not mean who was born first, who is oldest chronologically. It also does not mean that the youngest usurps the role of the oldest.

What God and Abraham, Isaac and Jacob are conveying is that the firstborn status is *available and accessible* to each child in each family. The firstborn status reflects each person's covenantal relationship with God and the inheritance of spirituality along with earthly possessions. Each child in each family is constantly reminded of this by the blessing given, "May God make you as Ephraim and Menasheh."

The parents' hope and prayer is that each child will be the firstborn, not in the concrete, or material way, but as the recipient of the familial spiritual mandate to be a blessing to God, our Patriarchs, our Matriarchs, our mothers and our fathers.

VII

AS JACOB DIES, HE IS KISSED BY HIS SON, JOSEPH

After Jacob feels he has prepared the path for the ultimate redemption, he dies at the age of 147.

The Bible states, seemingly unnecessarily, that "Joseph fell upon his father's face, cried and kissed his deceased father" (Genesis 50:1).

Joseph, the newly proclaimed firstborn, the dreamer, the man of vision, kissed his deceased father. Joseph knew intellectually that a deceased person has no feelings. Joseph also did not kiss Jacob out of guilt, feeling that perhaps he should have contacted his father during the twenty-two year period that he was absent from home. Joseph knew and felt intuitively that his entire life was guided by a special Divine Providence.

He kissed Jacob for a very spiritual and loving reason, because he knew that Jacob had not really died -- "Jacob, our father, has not died" (Talmud, *Taanit* 5b). Jacob continues to touch every child as that child is touched, kissed and embraced by his or her parents as they bless their children by saying, "May God make you as Ephraim and Menasheh."

Therefore, Joseph kissed his father as all sons kiss their fathers. And as all of us kiss our parents, we kiss Jacob as well. By receiving kisses from all his children, Jacob was healed during his lifetime, and he continues to live spiritually after his death. In this spiritual existence he continues to receive universal love and affection. Jacob, our forefather, lives as he blesses us and as we kiss him.

CHAPTER V

SECRETS OF THE HEART: JACOB'S BLESSINGS

I

INTRODUCTION

Jacob was the first person in Biblical history to become chronically ill. Everyone else is reported to have lived a healthy life and then died at a ripe old age. During Jacob's years of illness prior to his death, he contemplated and reflected upon his entire life, but primarily on what his final message would be to his children. He realized that this message would be profoundly personal, absolutely authentic, and that it would sustain not only his children and grandchildren, but also the entire Jewish people until the arrival of the Messianic era.

While on his deathbed, Jacob experienced a variety of feelings regarding death. A part of him anticipated death as a final release from his physical suffering and chronic illness. For Jacob, death would also be a release from his subjective experience of life, as he himself proclaimed, "few and evil have been the days of the years of my life" (Genesis 47:9). Another part of Jacob eagerly anticipated death as a spiritual gathering with his parents, Rebekah and Isaac, and his grandparents, Sarah and Abraham. Jacob's spiritual death is so described in a beautiful Biblical phrase, "And [Jacob] was gathered unto his people" (Genesis 49:33).

This phrase connotes the beginning of a new spiritual life after physical death. Jacob, a prophet during his lifetime (Genesis 28:15), yearned to be reunited with the *Shekhinah*, the Divine Presence. He felt that this eternal experience of being surrounded by the *Shekhinah* would be the ultimate experience. It would somehow create a new understanding of his entire earthly existence, including the pain and suffering he encountered with his parents, brothers, wives and children, as well as his struggles with changing Images of the Divine.

Jacob understood the meaning of his illness in both personal and collective terms. On a personal level, he realized that anyone who struggles genuinely with the Image of the Divine, anyone who experiences existential crises, anyone who experiences the lonely night journey of the soul, reflects those issues in the vessel of the soul, the body. Jacob similarly recognized that on the collective level, his future descendants would all be called Israel, the children who struggle, each one in his or her own path, with the multiple Images of God and the experiences of life.

Jacob had learned a new and profound understanding of life -- that all of life, body and soul, is one entity. The body reflects the soul, and the soul reflects the body. Emotional suffering, mental anguish, the wounded psyches of each individual, all find their mirror reflections in high blood pressure or some other symptom relating to the body's physical systems. Marital dissatisfaction, difficulty and stresses involved in raising children and taking care of elderly parents all take a physical toll on the body.

As Jacob was on his deathbed, about to bestow the final blessings on his children, the penultimate statement for the rest of time concerning the entire Jewish people, he first asked all of his children to gather together by his bedside. This first and, indeed, only such request was his essential message concerning how to arrive at the Messianic era.

Jacob employed an instructive word to assemble his sons, *"He-osfu,"* "gather yourselves together" (Genesis 49:1). Would it be possible for the eleven brothers to gather together with Joseph, who initially wore the coat of many colors, became the viceroy of Egypt, dreamt dreams and was almost murdered by his brothers? The eleven tribes of Israel almost committed fratricide. Their relationship with Benjamin was also filled with sibling rivalry, because he was their father's beloved soul mate (Genesis 44:30) and youngest son (Genesis 44:20). Reuben and Judah had distinct ideologies, different ways of looking at the world. Could each son transcend life's issues and gather together with his brethren in order to receive the paternal blessing?

They did gather together, with tears in their eyes and love in their souls. Each son transcended egotistical and ideological differences in this gathering process. By doing this, they paved the way for family reconciliation, a prerequisite for national reconciliation, which is the precursor to the Messianic era.

How was this reconciliation possible, considering that there had been a fraternal plot to murder the brother who dreamt and had visions? It was made possible by Joseph's perception of all the ills, animosities and hatred that he experienced. He interpreted his "victimization" as Divine Providence, as he expressly articulated on two separate occasions: "...for God did send me before you to preserve life" (Genesis 45:5; similarly, 50:20).

Joseph recognized that the journey of life, with its triumphs and tribulations, is unfathomable, but always under direct Divine guidance. Although the journey may never be understood, throughout it one needs to have adequate faith to sustain one through the difficulties, always anticipating the ultimate, meaningful culmination of the journey of life. Furthermore, Joseph understood that although the motivation of his brothers was evil -- to harm and then kill him -- all the "evil" that befell him was intentionally used by God for positive outcomes.

Thus, what the reconciliation meant for the Tribes and for all future generations was the recognition of the supremacy of Divine guidance over the evil intentions of human beings. Joseph also taught us to hold on to faith in God, even during times of trial and tribulation. Perhaps this teaching is the reason that Joseph is referred to in Rabbinic literature as the *Tzadik*, the righteous one.

His brothers also deserve credit for not holding on to old hatreds and points of contention. Situations change, new meanings are found, and new beginnings, with a heightened awareness of oneself and others, are always possible. This type of reconciliation is ultimately required for ushering in the Messianic era.

II

SECRETS OF THE HEART

Like every other human being, Jacob has multiple dimensions. There is his persona, "the whole man dwelling in tents," who meditates upon the mysteries of God and the world. At the same time, his psyche, wounded by his parents, manifests itself in his relationships with his brother, Esau; his four wives; his twelve sons and one daughter, and the world at large. However, deeper and more profound than Jacob's persona and the wounded and healthy parts of his psyche are the secrets of his heart, which ultimately are the determining factors of all the components of his heart.

Secrets of the heart are so personal and intimate that most people rarely articulate or verbally express them, except perhaps in a psychotherapeutic or analytical relationship. Even in these private relationships, secrets of the heart are shared only after a trusting relationship has emerged over a long period of time.

Each person's individual secrets are ultimately universal in nature, perhaps with slight variations. These universal secrets reflect the basic insecurity of each individual: Am I likable? Am I lovable? The skeletons in the closet are universal as well: an alcoholic father, incestuous family relationships, gambling, a suicide that is not spoken of, extreme forms of rage in interpersonal behavior, white-collar crimes, great obesity, unfaithfulness, drug problems, as well as chronic illnesses, both physical and emotional.

Jacob, who recognized all the personas of his children as well as his own, including the deep wounds and the universal secrets of the heart, wanted to share with his children, the Jewish people and all of humanity what will transpire until the "end of days," i.e., the Messianic era (Genesis 49:1). He desperately wanted to impart his belief that one day tears will turn into smiles; anxiety, despair, sadness, existential crises and all the negative things that have been experienced since the time of Adam will all be transformed into positive experiences. Men will understand women and vice versa. At last, there will be universal belief in One God.

However, God suddenly removed Jacob's prophetic vision of when the Messianic period would arrive.

> Our Rabbis said: "[Jacob] came to reveal to them the end [of days], and it was hidden from him." (Midrash, Genesis *Rabbah* 98 on Genesis 49)

Why did God prefer a world where the Messianic future was an unknown, rather than a known entity? I believe that what God taught Jacob and ultimately, all of the Children of Israel, is that more significant than the date, time and place of the ultimate redemption, is the journey itself, the process, the way. The goal is the journey itself. Constantly refining that process, sometimes falling, sometimes deviating intentionally or unintentionally from "the path" -- all of this is the goal of the journey.

This is how life is actually experienced. Anticipation, expectation and preparation for a major moment indeed create the moment, even before its arrival. Thus, as each person experiences challenges and difficulties, the ability to grow -- and even experience Divinity during the eclipse of God's face -- is the journey as well as its goal.

God's teaching to Jacob was that every plateau, as well as every achievement, becomes a stepping-stone to new development in everyone's life. The essence of life is continuous growth as one experiences constantly changing images of a personal God, dialogues with a personal God, develops oneself and has an impact on the world.

Many events in life have four stages: a birthing process, development of that process, a decaying process, and a form of death that gives rise to a new birthing process, thus starting the cycle anew. This is the journey of life, with each person improving or faltering along the way, since each human being incorporates the potential for both good and evil.

As a result of God's intervention, revealing to Jacob the journey and cycle of life, Jacob decided to help future generations by accentuating his own mistakes, as well as the mistakes and virtues of his children. The points that Jacob made in blessing his children epitomize central issues in everyone's life.

III

PRIVATE SEXUAL STRUGGLES

Jacob bestows his first blessing upon Reuben, his firstborn. It tells us as much about Jacob as it does about Reuben. Jacob shares more secrets about his life that are ultimately universal secrets. I would not have the audacity or be so presumptuous as to write about Jacob's secrets were it not for the fact that Jacob either states them directly or alludes to them indirectly.

Jacob says that the firstborn of his thirteen children (or Twelve Tribes) is Reuben, who was conceived with Leah from the first semen he ever emitted (Midrash, Genesis *Rabbah* 98 on Genesis 49). This is certainly an unusual statement; such a personal remark is not found in any other place in the entire Bible.

What was going on in Jacob's life until the conception of Reuben that first night, when he thought he was married to Rachel but found out in the morning that his first marriage was to Leah? Jacob was struggling, as each male and female does, with the limits and boundaries of normal sexual desires of single people. The desire for sexual union with a woman existed within Jacob's sexual fantasies.

Jacob was sure that he would not have sexual relations until he married. However, he struggled with his normal sexual fantasies, produced involuntarily by his psyche. Long before he met Rachel, he dreamt of a woman like her. In his dreams, she appeared in many different shapes, guises and forms. They united in his dreams and fantasies, but Jacob never intentionally masturbated. This self control presented an enormous struggle within his psyche.

Jacob wondered why God creates these normal, involuntary human desires. At the same time he recognized that semen is more than just a fluidic substance. Each sperm contains the potential for human life, imbued with the Image of God. Jacob's dreams and fantasies were continuous, but he, "the whole man dwelling in tents," was able to wait painfully and patiently until his first union with Rachel, who turned out to be Leah, in order to achieve the maximum purity of power and thought to produce his firstborn, Reuben. Reuben was born from a pure Jacob.

However, when the internal struggle is so enormous, and one abstains from emitting seed, always waiting for the right moment for this holy energy and act to occur, on some level one expects to be rewarded. A man may develop extremely high expectations for an easy and fulfilling life, for himself or for his children. Generally, one never speaks about these secret struggles and hopes.

The reality of life does not seem to resonate with one's religious commitment and lifestyle. That is why the central philosophical-religious issue of Judaism, as well as of other religions, is the eternal question of theodicy. A person who seemingly lives a righteous life sometimes does not experience the rewards for such a life, while a person who seemingly has intentionally deviated from the Divine path is rewarded with a good life. In a smaller dimension, this conundrum relates to Jacob's waiting and hoping for the right time to be intimate with his beloved and having so many wonderful expectations for his firstborn.

As Jacob's firstborn, Reuben was destined to become Jacob's priest (*kohen*) and king (Genesis 49:3). Thus, Jacob's lifelong dream and high expectations were fulfilled. But whenever there is an extreme, such as Jacob's explicit statement that Reuben's birth was the result of adhering to high sexual ethics, reflecting Jacob's struggle and hopes for a reward of some kind, life has a way of attenuating itself.

After Rachel died, Reuben, the firstborn son of Jacob and Leah, went to "visit" the tent of Bilhah, Jacob's concubine. Reuben's action was motivated by the fact that he was very upset that Jacob moved his bed next to Bilhah's after Rachel died, instead of moving it next to Leah's. So Reuben, out of anger that his mother, Leah, was still seemingly abandoned and embarrassed even after Rachel's death, visited Bilhah's tent, took Jacob's bed and placed it in Leah's tent.

> During all the time that Rachel was alive, her bed was placed next to the bed of Jacob, our forefather. After Rachel died, Jacob our forefather took Bilhah's bed and placed it next to his bed. (Midrash, Genesis *Rabbah* 98 on Genesis 49)

Exactly what took place between Reuben and his father's concubines is unclear. One Midrashic interpretation seems to imply that Reuben had intimate relations with *both* of his father's concubines, Bilhah and Zilpah.

> Rabbi Brakhia stated [Regarding Genesis 49:4]: "The text does not state 'the bed of your father,' but 'the beds of your father.' [This

refers to] the bed of Bilhah and the bed of Zilpah." (Midrash, Genesis *Rabbah* 98 on Genesis 49)

The Biblical text states that Reuben had sexual relations with Bilhah (Genesis 35:22). The Talmud states that he moved his father's bed to Leah's tent (*Shabbat* 55b). The Midrash contrasts Jacob's behavior with that of Reuben.

> You are a firstborn, and I am a firstborn. I was 84 years old, and I had not emitted a drop of semen. But you went and slept with Bilhah. (Midrash, Genesis *Rabbah* 98 on Genesis 49)

The Midrashic version is especially poignant because of Jacob's statement regarding his being a firstborn. Surely that must have brought to mind, both for him and his children, the early years of his life, when he acquired the birthright through deception. His name, Jacob, always connoted that deceptive element of his persona, while his alternate name, Israel, reflected his struggle with God. Perhaps it also connoted Israel's struggle with the part of his nature that is, for all humans, the most "God-like" -- the ability to procreate and produce new life.

Whatever actually took place in the incident involving Reuben is less significant than the fact that Jacob's firstborn, born from the first sperm that Jacob ever emitted in his life, destined to become the priest and king of the family, committed an impropriety with his father's wives. For this act, Jacob, while on his deathbed, said to Reuben that all three titles would be removed from him. The status of firstborn would go to Joseph, the priesthood would go to Levi, and the kingship would be transferred to Judah.

> The status of firstborn was yours, and the priesthood was yours, and the kingship was yours. And now that you have sinned, the status of firstborn has been given to Joseph, the priesthood has gone to Levi, and the kingship to Judah. (Midrash, Genesis *Rabbah* 98 on Genesis 49)

The power of Jacob's statement to Reuben requires elaboration. Why did Jacob remove the three great roles originally intended for Reuben?

What blessing did Jacob want to bestow on all future generations of the Jewish people?

IV

THE PRIVACY OF THE BRIDAL CHAMBER

I believe that Jacob wanted to teach two essential principles regarding marital and family life. National Jewish life is dependent upon family and marital life. By reprimanding Reuben in stating, "you went up to your father's beds" (Genesis 49:4), Jacob prophesied what Balaam would eventually say about the Jewish people: "How beautiful are your *tents*, O Jacob, your sanctuaries, O Israel!" (Numbers 24:5).

In those words, Balaam referred to the beautiful intimacy between husband and wife, which will always be the paradigm for intimacy between male and female. How interesting it is that Balaam highlights this concept by referring to Jacob's *tents*. Even in the midst of their desert travels, the Israelites maintained the privacy and dignity of their individual families in their mobile *tents*. Furthermore, the privacy of marriage is so essential that no one else -- no parent, no child, no brother or sister -- can ever enter the eternal bridal chamber of husband and wife.

Jacob knew that if the marital union is paramount, if the masculine and feminine are united in total intimacy, where vulnerabilities are shared, the result can be a transformation into a special kind of love. This love creates the foundation for a healthy family life. What Reuben did, regardless of his motivation -- to protect his mother, Leah, from feeling rejected and abandoned -- was a violation of the *chuppah*, the marital canopy, which contains invisible walls that surround the couple all the days of their lives. Interestingly, it is not clear whether Reuben *himself* was married at the time of the incident with Bilhah. Only a listing of Reuben's children (Genesis 46:9) shows that he, in fact, was married.

Jacob looked at the entire Jewish people as his personal family. Therefore, his rebuke of Reuben served as a blessing for the entire Jewish people. All of Jacob's blessings, which revealed the secrets of Jacob's heart, including the anger that was never before articulated, became blessings for the entire Jewish people for all generations.

What was Jacob's immediate reaction to the episode between Reuben and Bilhah? Perhaps a clue can be found in the punctuation of the relevant sentence (Genesis 35:22). Every Biblical sentence has cantillation marks (*te'amim*) that generally include both a pause in the middle (*etnahta*), and an indication of the end of the sentence (*sof pasuk*). Only one sentence in the Bible (Genesis 35:22) has an empty space after the *etnahta*. The verse states: "And it came to pass, while Israel dwelt in that land, that Reuben went and lay with his father's concubine; *and Israel heard of it* [*Va-yishma Yisrael*]...now the sons of Jacob were twelve." The empty space indicates that the verse pauses in the middle of the sentence.

This punctuation may indicate that Jacob wanted to deliberate about how to use his pain and anguish. Rather than responding immediately, he paused and pondered how to use this tremendous disappointment with his firstborn by transforming it into a blessing for the Jewish people.

Jacob was able to transcend his immediate ego and eventually respond from a transcendent place, his Higher Self. This response serves as a very noble lesson for generations to come, i.e., not to respond impulsively or instinctively. Allow events and stimuli to be absorbed. Allow your soul to taste them, experience them, dream about them, digest them, dialogue with them, and amplify them, and then, at an appropriate time, articulate your response.

I suggest that Jacob was also teaching future generations that the phrase, "*Shema Yisrael*" ("Hear, O Israel"), meant to temper one's response, would ultimately become the Jewish declaration of faith as expressed in "*Hear, O Israel, the Eternal our God, the Eternal is One*" (Deuteronomy 6:4). Interestingly, Jacob was comforted on his deathbed, before bestowing the blessings, when his children told their father in unison that they would continue the religious values that he developed during his lifetime. They said "*Shema Yisrael*," "*Hear, O Israel*, our Father, just as your heart is complete and one with the Holy One Blessed Be He, so in our hearts there is total accord that *the Eternal our God, the Eternal is One*" (Midrash, Genesis *Rabbah* 98:3; Talmud, *Pesahim*, 56a).

Jacob's major rebuke of Reuben raises another significant issue in Jacob's life as it compares to the life of his father, Isaac, and his grandfather, Abraham. The Bible states (Genesis 33:18) that Jacob is considered the most complete Patriarch, since Abraham also gave birth to Ishmael, and Isaac gave birth to Esau. By contrast, Jacob gave birth to the future Twelve Tribes of Israel, i.e., all of Jacob's children followed in his Godly path.

However, based on Reuben's actions, Jacob rebukes him and eliminates his three hereditary titles of firstborn, priest and king. It seems, *prima facie*, that Jacob is similar to Isaac and Abraham in that he produced a child like Reuben, who violated the essential basis of intimate holiness between husband and wife.

The essence of a child is not determined by focusing on one enormous mistake. Reuben is just like everyone else who struggles to live a virtuous life. Reuben and every other individual are ultimately judged by their actions when they realize they have made mistakes. How does Reuben receive the rebuke, and what does he do with it? Does he ignore it, or does he really change his life?

Jacob is not the only one who blesses the Twelve Tribes. Moses blesses them in his farewell speech, stating that "Reuben lives" (Deuteronomy 33:6), an expression demonstrating that God is with Reuben. From this statement, it is clear that Reuben repented throughout his lifetime for the error that he committed.

Consequently, Reuben not only redeemed himself, but also elevated himself to an even higher level of holiness. As the Talmud states (*Berakhot* 34b), people who repent from a grievous sin are on a much different level than people who have never sinned. As a result of Reuben's process of repentance, in every place that the Bible enumerates the Twelve Tribes, it states that Reuben is the firstborn of his father, Jacob. The role of firstborn was given to Joseph, but it also was retained for Reuben whenever he is mentioned with all his brothers (e.g., Exodus 6:14; Numbers 1:20, etc.).

V

THE OEDIPUS COMPLEX

For the act for which Reuben was strongly rebuked, Jacob wanted to hand down an additional, essential teaching other than the importance of intimacy between husband and wife. The second lesson addresses an aspect of humanity that was rediscovered by Sigmund Freud thousands of years later.

By being intimate with Bilhah or by moving Jacob's bed near his mother's bed, Reuben, Jacob's eldest, was expressing what Freud would later call the Oedipus complex, a son's desire to take over his father's role and want his father's wife for himself.

Oedipus, a figure in a play by Sophocles, unknowingly murdered his father and married his mother. Freud claimed that a boy develops a sexual interest in his mother and competitive aggression toward his father. As the boy realizes that his father is larger and stronger, he learns to identify with his father and to shift his own sexual interests to someone other than his mother.

Freud further asserted that little girls experience an Electra complex, named after a character in an ancient Greek play who persuades her brother to kill their mother, who had murdered their father. A girl with an Electra complex feels a romantic attraction toward her father and hostility toward her mother.

The family dynamic of the Oedipus complex was expressed very succinctly in Jacob's rebuke of Reuben: "For you invaded the sexual privacy of your father" (Genesis 49:4). Jacob recognized that it is a normal sexual desire for a son to replace his father and be intimate with his mother or one of his father's other "wives." But Jacob teaches that one should not act out this desire. Recognize the struggle, heighten the awareness, dialogue with the complexity of all of these feelings, but do not actually act on these impulses.

Jacob further said that the blessing for all generations is to deepen our understanding of human behavior and family dynamics through heightened consciousness, which can overcome human instinctual behavior. In other words, these patterns will repeat themselves unless families and individuals recognize the desires and yearnings that exist within everyone as normal.

Jacob's first blessing for future generations deals with three aspects of sexuality: Jacob's self-restraint with his sexual fantasies, so that his first semen produced his firstborn son; the inviolate sanctity of the intimacy between husband and wife, both sexual and spiritual; and the inappropriate sexual family enmeshments of a son desiring to replace his father and to be intimate with his mother.

Thus, the first blessing deals with the enormous desires in the area of human sexuality. Jacob asks the Jewish people to become more aware of sexual issues and their importance for the well-being of an individual. Jacob set the foundation for individual and family sexual development.

Sexuality represents the highest form of communication between two individuals. In this form of communication, it is not adequate to relate as the persona, such as the "whole man dwelling in tents." Nor is it adequate to relate sexually based on one's wounded psyche, common to all of humanity. Rather, Jacob says that intimate communication in the form of human sexuality must reveal the secrets of the hearts, the universal secrets of humanity, thereby revealing the complex struggle and duality of being human.

This lesson involves the intense struggle of experiencing oneself with all the diametrically opposed forces within: on the one hand, the good tendency, the openness, the sharing, the vulnerabilities, the universal secrets; on the other, the evil tendency and the concealed parts of the heart.

These feelings were some of the secrets of Jacob's heart throughout his lifetime, and the message that he wanted to deliver to the Jewish people. When the Jewish people can develop to such an extent that they can relate to one another based on the universal secrets of the heart, the Messianic era will gradually be ushered in.

VI

JACOB'S SPIRITUAL LEGACY AND THE DEATH OF ABRAHAM

Another secret of Jacob's heart needed to be clarified for the Jewish people. When Jacob looked at Reuben and said, "you are my firstborn" (Genesis 49:3), he was looking, in one respect, at his mirror reflection. But he remained perplexed. He denigrated Reuben by proclaiming inwardly, "we are both firstborns, but there is a big difference between you and me. I was 84 years old when I married, and on that first night when I was together with my wife, my first semen was emitted, but you, Reuben, did not behave that way" (Midrash, Genesis *Rabbah* 98 on Genesis 49).

One person's denigration of another is often based on deep-seated feelings of inadequacy. Jacob denigrated Reuben in part because Jacob knew that Reuben was a chronological firstborn, just like Jacob's twin, Esau. Jacob was still bothered by how he acquired the status of firstborn.

Jacob recalled the entire episode. He was born a twin, who entered this world after Esau, the chronological firstborn. When the brothers were 15 years old (Talmud, *Bava Batra* 16b), events occurred that would change their destinies (Genesis 25:29-34).

One day, Jacob was preparing a dish and letting it simmer while Esau returned from the field. Presumably, Esau had been out hunting and was exhausted. As Esau saw the delicious red lentil soup on the fire, he asked Jacob if he might have some, because he was extremely hungry and thirsty. In response, Jacob asked to buy the birthright from Esau, seemingly in exchange for the soup. Esau felt famished, so he sold his birthright through an oath that he made to his brother Jacob. Jacob fulfilled his promise and gave Esau bread and lentil soup, and Esau left. Esau thought so little of his birthright that he preferred the immediate gratification of soup over the privilege of being the firstborn.

The method by which Jacob obtained the birthright immediately calls into question how a "whole man dwelling in tents" can prey on the vulnerability of his brother, taking advantage of harsh circumstances.

Jacob's action seems almost to resemble the action of the Amalekites, who attacked the faint, tired and weary Children of Israel on their way out of Egypt. The same Hebrew word, *ayef*, meaning "fatigued," is used both to describe Esau at the time he requested the lentil soup (Genesis 25:30,31) and the Children of Israel at the time of the Amalekite attack (Deuteronomy 25:18).

What is the fundamental meaning of being a *bekhor* (firstborn)? Does it depend merely on birth order? Apparently not. Why was Jacob cooking lentil soup, and why does the Bible describe this activity? The Rabbis interpreted Jacob's act as preparing a meal of condolence, symbolized by lentils, for his father, because on that day Abraham, Isaac's father and Jacob's grandfather, had died (Genesis 25:8; Talmud, *Bava Batra* 16b).

On the day that their grandfather died, Jacob and Esau performed very different activities. Jacob consoled and helped his father, while Esau committed five grievous sins. He had illicit sexual relations with a young, engaged woman; he killed someone; he publicly denied the resurrection of the dead; he denied the existence of God; and he denigrated the status of the firstborn (Midrash, Genesis *Rabbah* 63 on Genesis 25:29-34).

Jacob realized that the spiritual legacy of his grandfather, Abraham, had been given to Isaac, his father, and not to Ishmael, his uncle, who was the older brother. This special legacy that Isaac had received was not to be given to Esau, but rather to Jacob, who could be trusted to safeguard it. Esau, who committed five grievous sins in one day, was not ready to serve as the spiritual firstborn. Therefore, Jacob took advantage of Esau's hunger and fatigue in order to purchase the title of spiritual heir.

Esau was not ready to sacrifice his immediate gratification. Impulsively, he decided to forego his privileged rank of firstborn. Nevertheless, no matter how lofty Jacob's motives were in his purchase of the birthright, he wanted, I believe, to teach future generations an important lesson. There are times or special circumstances when deception can be necessary, desired and even holy.

Jacob, the seemingly "whole person dwelling in tents," really understood that sometimes the goal is so significant that the process may involve less than ideal truth in order to accomplish the goal. Life is never a straight line. Deviation from the path may be necessary in order to ensure that the paternal blessing will be secure for all future generations.

As a result of Jacob's acquisition of the status of spiritual firstborn, he knew that Reuben could not continue that special, spiritual legacy. What Reuben did took place immediately following Rachel's death. What Esau did took place on the day that Abraham died. One's reactions to the death of a Matriarch or Patriarch are often very significant. Death is, at times, a liberating catalyst for offspring. The younger person can now freely choose the path on which to continue.

Possessing this insight and understanding, Jacob bestowed his blessing on Reuben. Before Jacob's death, he called his sons together and said:

> Gather together in unity so that I may share with you the process of striving for continuous self-improvement until we finally arrive at the Messianic era. Assemble yourselves and listen to Jacob, or Israel, your father.
>
> Reuben, you are my firstborn, you are the product of my strength and the very first issue from my semen. You were also worthy of being the High Priest and King. However, you have been unstable as water and therefore, the distinction of being firstborn, High Priest and King will be withdrawn from you. This consequence is a result of your improper actions regarding your father's bed and Bilhah, whereby you defiled the Divine Presence on your father's bed. (Genesis 49)

In essence, Jacob's blessing of Reuben focuses on the pivotal role of sexuality in the lives of individuals and communities. Jacob recognizes that his own internal struggles, as well as those of Reuben, are common to all of humanity. Therefore, Jacob addresses key issues, such as how unmarried people struggle with normal sexual desires and fantasies; how family sexual tensions and enmeshments are common to everyone; and how sexual fantasies, privacy and secrets of the psyche are necessary components of the human condition. The internalization of Jacob's teachings and insights leads to a recognition and awareness that sexuality can be a spiritual and sacred part of life.

CONCLUSION

Not only does Jacob, our father, still live, but so does his beloved wife, Rachel, our mother. Although she died tragically while giving birth to Benjamin, her second son, Rachel continues to watch over, protect, nurture and nourish all of Jacob's descendants.

At times, Rachel cries, passionately yearning for and anticipating the ingathering of the exiles and the ultimate redemption of her people (Jeremiah 31:14-16). At other times, in her most feminine, exquisite, beautiful and charming way, Rachel continuously gives birth, sustains hope and promotes creativity in each of us.

Rachel's tears and sadness represent not only her *personal*, unfulfilled life, not only her lost love-life with her beloved Jacob, not only her death in childbirth, not only being unable to be a mother to Benjamin at all, or to Joseph for longer than seventeen years; but also, and essentially, her sadness encompasses the *collective* feelings of all her future children, all of us throughout the millennia, whose individual lives are marked with pain, suffering, anguish and unfulfilled yearnings.

Rachel's tears are only a part of her legacy. Her feminine beauty, the beauty of her soul mirrored in her ravishingly beautiful physical appearance, empowers each one of us with new visions and hope when, at times, the challenges of life seem insurmountable.

When Jacob was in Rachel's presence, both during her lifetime and afterwards, when he imagined and dialogued with her, Rachel empowered him, enabling him to recreate himself and give birth to new aspects of his soul as he traveled along his difficult life journey. During Jacob's moments of despair, the image of Rachel brought him understanding, consolation and comfort. As his pain subsided, Jacob felt increasingly nurtured and nourished.

CONCLUSION

These reflections on Jacob and his family, and on the dialogue between his internal and external selves, leave Jacob and all of us with insight into one of the central issues of our lives. Although God promised Jacob that he would never abandon him, Jacob's life was full of anguish. Such is the universal experience of life. Even with God's presence, life is often turbulent and challenging. What does the complex nature of life teach us about our individual lives and, ultimately, about the unfathomable Divine Image?

The journey of life requires that each individual experience a continuing birthing process. Biological birth is only our first transformative experience. Life involves ongoing renewal, essential for our emotional, psychological, social, spiritual and physical development. This process requires a continuous *dialogue* with our changing Images of God.

When Jacob feared meeting his brother, he clearly stated that he was greatly afraid (Genesis 32:8), and he subsequently asked for strength and courage. After Job experienced the pain and torment of his life, he cursed the day that he was born (Job 3:1). Jacob and Job each maintained a *relationship* with the Image of God that they were experiencing at a particular moment. Jacob contended with immediate fear for his physical safety, while Job grappled with the fear of life's meaninglessness. Job pondered how a pious, God-fearing individual can be subjected to terrible physical and emotional illness and loss.

From these and similar episodes, we learn that the life-cycle developmental process involves a continuing dialogue with the self about what one is experiencing, and sharing those moments with God. Thus, a religious life involves maintaining a relationship with God through *dialogue*, whereby each person continually gains new insights into life. This sharing leads to a heightened awareness of ourselves, the changing Images of God and our relationship with God.

In this way, everyone's life journey is unique and distinct. Ultimate, universal "answers" do not exist. However, in the ongoing process of "rebirth," we find out who we are and how we relate personally to God.

Both Jacob and Rachel still live, each one empowering and enabling us to recognize the complex nature of our lives, to dialogue with God and to relate to God. We establish new paradigms and shifts in our psyche, often as a consequence of physical illness, emotional illness or a death in the family. As we confront new, and sometimes difficult, situations and events, our internal attitudes and relationships with the Divine continue to change.

Ultimately, we can arrive at a stage where our every feeling, thought, action, and interpersonal relationship becomes a form of prayer to God. Our whole life will then become a continuing prayer to God.

REFERENCES

Altman, Erwin. (1987). Excerpts from Reflections on this Thing and No-Thing called Life and Death. *Journal of Psychology and Judaism*, *11* (2), edited by L. Meier. Reprinted in L. Meier, *Jewish values in psychotherapy: Essays on vital issues on the search for meaning*. (1988). Lanham, Md.: University Press of America.

Altmann, Adolf (Avraham). (1928). Sinn und Seele des "Hore Israel." ("The Meaning and Soul of 'Hear, O Israel'"). Berlin: *Jeschurun* (ed. by Joseph Wohlgemuth), *11/12*. Translated from the German by Barbara R. Algin and edited by Levi Meier. In L. Meier, *Jewish values in Jungian psychology*. (1991). Lanham, Md.: University Press of America.

Frankl, V. (1984). *Man's search for meaning*. Rev. and updated. New York: Pocket Books.

The Holy Scriptures. (2 vols.) (1917). Philadelphia: Jewish Publication Society.

Maimonides, M. (1974). *The Guide of the perplexed*. Chicago: The University of Chicago Press.

Meier, L. (1991). *Jewish values in Jungian psychology*. Lanham, Md.: University Press of America.

Midrash. (10 vols.) (1961). H. Freedman and M. Simons (Eds.). London: Soncino Press.

Midrash. *Sifrei on Numbers* [Hebrew] (1966). Horovitz ed. Jerusalem: Wahrmann.

The Talmud. (18 vols.) (1961). I. Epstein (Ed.). London: Soncino Press.

JACOB

ABOUT THE AUTHOR

Levi Meier was born in New York in 1946. After receiving Rabbinical ordination from Yeshiva University of New York, he completed a Ph.D. in psychology at the University of Southern California. He is a licensed Marriage, Family and Child Counselor, as well as a Clinical Psychologist.

Dr. Meier's academic training was supplemented by his own Jungian analysis. As Chaplain at Cedars-Sinai Medical Center in Los Angeles, CA, Rabbi Meier serves as a catalyst in the healing process of patients and their families. His work as Chaplain focuses on pastoral counseling and medical ethics. Also, in his private practice as a clinical psychologist, Dr. Meier enables clients to draw upon their inner resources in their own process of healing.

Dr. Meier is the creator of the *Jewish Values* series, which so far includes: *Jewish Values in Bioethics, Jewish Values in Psychotherapy, Jewish Values in Health and Medicine* and *Jewish Values in Jungian Psychology*. Rabbi Meier is also Special Issues Editor of the *Journal of Psychology and Judaism*.

Levi Meier continues to teach numerous classes on psychology and Judaism. He also supervises Rabbinical students in pastoral counseling and trains psychology interns in analytic psychotherapy.

Dr. Meier continues to explore new ways of enriching his creative imagination, such as meditation, breathing exercises and art projects. He, his wife, Marcie, and their four children reside in Beverly Hills, California.

GENERAL THEOLOGICAL SEMINARY
NEW YORK

DATE DUE			
JAN 03 1997			
MAR 20 1997			
DEC 16 1998			
MAY 17 1999			
APR 24 2001			
JAN 02 2006			